D1058264

WHAT DO YOU MEAN, YOU CAN'T EAT IN MY HOME?

A Guide to

How Newly Observant Jews

and Their Less-Observant Relatives

Can Still Get Along

AZRIELA JAFFE

SCHOCKEN BOOKS, NEW YORK

WHAT DO YOU MEAN, YOU CAN'T EAT IN MY HOME?

Library of Congress Cataloging-in-Publication Data

Jaffe, Azriela.

What do you mean, you can't eat in my home?: a guide to how newly observant Jews and their less-observant relatives can still get along / Azriela Jaffe.

p. cm.

ISBN 0-8052-4221-X

1. Jewish families—Religious life. 2. Orthodox Judaism—Relations—Nontraditional Jews. 3. Jews—Return to Orthodox Judaism. 4. Judaism—Customs and practices. I. Title.

BM725.J345 2005 296.7—dc22 2004065345

www.schocken.com

Printed in the United States of America

First Edition

2 4 6 8 9 7 5 3 1

I dedicate this book to my parents, Maude and Phil Ackerman, who have finally accepted the fact that I'm not going to "get over this Orthodox thing." We couldn't be more different in our approaches to Judaism, but we are family and we love one another. Mom and Dad, to the rest of the world I am Azriela. To you I will always be Linda, my birth name, and that's okay.

I also dedicate this book to my ancestors, all the multi-great grandparents going back to Sinai. I imagine that you are smiling from shomayim. I have returned. I know you've been waiting.

CONTENTS

ACKNOWLEDGMENTS

I gratefully acknowledge and thank—

Rabbi Reuven Drucker, Rav of Agudath Israel of Edison/ Highland Park, New Jersey, who meticulously reviewed the manuscript and made suggestions that improved it enormously. Thank you for your close attention to both halachic details and matters of style, and for guiding our family on a daily basis.

Rabbi Alan Ullman, Rabbi Yitzchok Feldheim, Rabbi Yehudah Shemtov, Rabbi Aryeh Weinstein, Adina Henderson, Roiza Weinrich, Naomi Franklin, the lecturers at Gateways Seminars, the teachers at Partners in Torah, and many other valued Torah teachers over the past decade.

The audiences I addressed when speaking about my book *Two Jews Can Still Be a Mixed Marriage: Reconciling the Differences Regarding Religion in Your Marriage*. You kept asking me when I was going to write this book, because you needed it. Here it is!

My dedicated and passionate editor at Schocken Books,

Altie Karper, who cared about this book almost as much as I did, and made sure that it was published.

My parents, brothers, and sisters-in-law, for tolerating the tension that at times has entered our family because of my decision to live a Torah-observant lifestyle.

My beloved husband of twelve years, Stephen, who is always my confidante, backbone, and friend. We're doing this journey together, thank God. I am so lucky to be your wife.

My children, Sarah, Elana, and Elijah, for giving me my most important inspiration for becoming a Torah-observant Jew. Most people think I became observant because I married their daddy. The truth is, it was my children's love of Torah Judaism and God that propelled me down this road, and it is my deep and abiding love for them that has kept me on this road even when I was tempted to bolt.

Hashem, for giving us the Torah, for helping me appreciate its power and wisdom, and for giving me the teachers I needed when I was open to learning from them. Thank You as well for blessing me and my family with good health. With Your bracha, may this book reach the people who can benefit from its guidance.

INTRODUCTION

"HOW WOULD I BE ABLE TO . . ."

I would be a wealthy woman if I had a dollar for every time I either heard someone start a question with these words or used them myself to ask a question of my rabbi. It always begins the same way—"How would I be able to . . ."—and goes on to ask how an observant Jew can participate in an event involving less- or nonobservant family members while making sure that Jewish law is not violated *and* that the relatives are not offended. This issue comes up with every family simchah, or family get-together, more frequently than you would imagine. "How would I be able to eat in my mother's nonkosher kitchen?" "How would I be able to attend my niece's bat mitzvah in a Reform synagogue?" "How would I be able to join my extended family for the seder?"

The sentiment behind the questions, regardless of the family or the particular issue at hand, is always the same. The newly observant Jew says, or feels, something like this:

"I believe in the divine origin of the Torah—both the Written and Oral Law. And I believe that I must follow these laws as Jews have done for thousands of years before me, without adding to or subtracting from them. But I also love my family and I know they love me, and I know that one of the Ten Commandments is to honor my father and mother. Family is what anchors all of Jewish life. How can I live a Torah-observant life but still maintain relationships with my non- or less-observant parents, siblings, and extended family? Must I choose between being a part of my family and being a Torah-observant Jew? Is this really what God intended, for us to observe laws that have the potential to break apart families and cause everyone great pain? Isn't there some way that I can be an observant Jew and still be a member of my family?"

I am a ba'alas teshuvah: a Jew who was raised in a secular, nonobservant Jewish home and who as an adult chose to live a Torah-observant life. My story is hardly unique. I was raised in New York, on Long Island, among thousands of other Jews who celebrated their Jewishness with the annual hour-long Passover Seder. I attended the synagogue on the two "required" days of the year and celebrated Chanukah, sometimes with presents signed "Love, Santa." And that was it. My parents' friends were Jewish, and I knew I was a Jew, mostly because I knew I wasn't a Christian—the only other alternative. I felt Jewish, but I never felt like I was a member of a religion, because there was never any discussion of God or Torah in our home. Judaism was a culture, an ethnicity, a tribe to which I belonged. I was part of the Jewish people. Whatever thoughts about God my parents might have held privately they never shared with me or my siblings.

Like many girls back then, I didn't receive a Hebrew education. I watched my brothers become bar mitzvah with big parties, and no explanation was ever extended to me for why I didn't have a similar celebration. When I was growing up, girls didn't have bat mitzvahs—that came years later. Because I never went to Hebrew school and because my parents never discussed religious thoughts or issues in our home, I grew up with no knowledge whatsoever of the Torah, just like thousands of my peers.

To their great credit, my parents worked hard and achieved their American dream. They assimilated well into American society and provided me with an excellent education and a nice, middle-class home, thanks to both my mother's and father's successes in business. Most important—and not to be taken for granted nowadays—they created a strong, loving, and stable marriage, which formed the basis for the stable and loving family life they provided for me and my brothers. I don't recall whether our fence was a white picket one, but we grew up in a good neighborhood with an assortment of family dogs, piano lessons, summer camp (although never a Jewish one), and many of the privileges that accompany middle-class success.

Like many Jews of my generation, I spent my twenties peering into practically every religion but Judaism, trying to find God, assuming that God was to be found anywhere but in my own backyard. Torah? What was that? But I didn't find God in the ashrams or in New Age practices, although I certainly tried. I never could bring myself to search for Him in any of the Christian sects, although I knew there were Jews who did. Eventually, through sheer good fortune and a whole lot of experimentation and persistence on my part, I stumbled across a few pivotal teachers and mentors who guided me back to choosing Judaism as my spiritual path. Rabbi Alan Ullman of Boston, Massachusetts, was the first rabbi who showed me the beauty and power of Torah. Under his guidance, for the first time in my life, I came to love being a Jew for reasons other than mere ethnicity. But it would still be a very long time—ten years—before I would become convinced that the Torah was the direct word of God, and that it was something I should follow.

I came to the decision to be an Orthodox Jew slowly. I started taking on religious practices in my early thirties, but I didn't feel ready to make a solid commitment to Yiddishkeit and an Orthodox lifestyle until I was in my early forties. In 1999, I wrote my eighth book and my first Jewish-oriented one, *Two Jews Can Still Be a Mixed Marriage: Reconciling Differences over Judaism in Your Marriage,* when my husband, Stephen, and I were negotiating disagreements regarding religious observance that began before our wedding. Over the course of our years together, after much study on my part and as a result of a few pivotal moments—such as our attending a Gateways seminar that opened my eyes to Torah in a whole new way—Stephen and I made a mutual commitment to living and raising our children as Torah-observant Jews. I came to this decision kicking and screaming at first, mostly prodded by Stephen, who was also a ba'al teshuvah but one who was more devoted to observance than I was at the time. The early years of our marriage were characterized by my muttering "You want me to do what?!" in reply to my husband's continuing requests that I take on more observant practices in our marriage and our home.

As I slowly traveled down the path from secular and unaffiliated to committed Reform, Conservative, and, eventually, Orthodox Jew, I found myself being transformed from an unwilling and resistant hostage to a true partner, as committed as Stephen was to raising our three children in an observant household. Throughout this ten-year journey, my parents and extended family watched, worried, and then hoped that I would get over this phase and return to "normal."

My mom, dad, and two younger brothers endured my changing my given name of Linda to a Hebrew name, Azriela. They were invited as guests to my adult bat mitzvah service when I was active in a Reform temple and decided to celebrate that ritual. They adjusted to my not coming home for the annual Passover Seder (the one religious ritual my family never missed) because their abbreviated Seder just didn't work for my husband and me anymore. They swallowed their hurt feelings when I spent half of a weekend visit with my brother's Sabbath-observant neighbor because everyone in my family spent that Saturday afternoon attending a ball game, shopping, and watching television, and I couldn't be with them and still keep Shabbos.

When Israel was struck repeatedly by terrorists, my mother worried that, now that I was observant, I might get the crazy idea to move to Israel. My family didn't attend my son's upsherin—his first haircut—because they just couldn't celebrate such an odd ritual with us. I know it was very hard for them at first to see my son's tzitzis and peyos, public symbols of being an observant Jew that he wears proudly, because they were raised to hide such flagrant displays of Jewish observance. They eventually stopped calling us during the Sabbath because they realized that we just wouldn't answer the phone, and we all got used to the ritual of checking in with one another on Friday afternoon, before the Sabbath.

My new religious practices and commitments are as alien to my family as if I had chosen to convert to another religion. I know that at times it seems to them as if I've gone off the deep end. But early on in my religious journey, I decided that I would not leave my family behind. I love my parents and my brothers. They are committed Jews—to the Reform Judaism that they know, love, and take pride in—and although they don't join me in my level of observance, I know that they love and respect me. I never proselytize or pressure them in any way to join me in increased observance. I don't ridicule or lecture them, or try to convince them to follow my way of observance. I have always understood that this is not my role. I love them for who they are, and I respect them.

I have over the years done everything I can to honor and respect my family and to stay connected to them, while at the same time moving away from the secular lifestyle that they find comfortable and that I now feel is incompatible and at cross purposes with my observant lifestyle. This is a very difficult path to walk. And so that's when the "How would I be able to . . ." questions arise, because I am always searching for room within Jewish law to do the halachically right thing but still keep connected to my extended family.

Orthodox rabbis with whom I have studied and whom I have consulted have surprised me on many occasions. While I knew that they would be concerned about what I ate, I was encouraged to see that they were also acutely attuned to human relationships and concerned with helping me achieve harmony in my family. There were a few times when I worried that the requirements of halachah would result in my having to do something that would be hurtful to my family and would strain the tenuous ties we had. But more often the surprise ran the other way—there were accommodations that could be made, within the halachic framework, that would allow me to be a part of my relatives' lives in ways that I did not think were possible. For example, I was genuinely shocked to discover that, by following certain rules, I could eat in my mother's non-kosher home. Which is to say, I could follow halachic requirements and at the same time maintain shalom bayis, or family harmony.

More often than not, my rabbis showed me how I possibly *could* do something, rather than flatly insisting that there was *no* way that I could. They demonstrated to me that I could be an observant Jew, fully committed to halachah, without separating entirely from my immediate family and my extended relatives. They destroyed the myth I once held that the ideal was to leave as far behind as possible my secular upbringing. They taught me to see it as a valued foundation, and that family connections are still worth holding on to.

NO ONE EVER SAID IT WOULD BE EASY

Shalom bayis in a family whose members are at different levels of observance is possible, but that doesn't mean it's easy. In my own journey, hundreds of questions and concerns have arisen along the way, on both sides. My family and I have hurt one another's feelings, made one another angry, and questioned one another's values, commitments, and priorities. But at least we are still very much a family, all of us doing our parts to maintain family harmony. There are plenty of days when I wish they would "see the light" and come along on my journey with me. On just as many days, they wish that I would calm down and return to their level of observance so that I could eat in their home without all the advance planning, join them in their synagogue, and stop doing weird things like wearing a wig all the time.

But more often now we are working out new ways to be together rather than reconciling ourselves to situations that move us farther apart. To my family's credit, they have, I believe, accepted my commitment and no longer think that it's something I'll "get over." They may even, on occasion, see the beauty in some of the things that I do, even if they don't choose to join me in doing them.

I wrote this book to create something that would explain to the relatives of newly observant Jews—including, of course, my parents, siblings, and extended family—the rationale behind the practices and beliefs of observant Jews, so that they would understand that what seems like a direct rejection of their way of life is really motivated by values and beliefs that they can appreciate, and even admire. And I hope that newly observant Jews—the "you" whom I address throughout the book—will find this book useful; that they will consult it themselves and perhaps even give it to their relatives when the questions and difficult times come. I have tried to create a text that answers the most common questions that newly observant Jews like me and my husband confront as we attempt to bring together two different worlds: that of our families of origin and that of our other family—the community of Torah-observant Jews.

The Torah doesn't claim that relationships between family members are easy or free of conflict. Quite the opposite is reflected in our ancestral heritage. But one thing has always been true: Isolation is not regarded as the ultimate form of holiness. And connections to God are to be found within our relationships with spouses, children, parents, and siblings. We can achieve through family relationships levels of holiness that can be found in no other place.

The newly observant Jew who exclaims, "My family is an obstacle to my spiritual growth!" may wish to rethink that statement. No better way exists for you to become a compassionate, patient, loyal, Torah-observant Jew than by succeeding in overcoming the family conflict that may arise because of your religious practices and beliefs.

The less- or nonobservant parent who exclaims, "My child's religious observance is undermining our family relationship!" may also wish to rethink that statement. We tend to take family relationships for granted. Family members can spend hours together, with the conversation barely extending beyond "Please pass the remote control" and "What's for dinner?" The Jewish family forced to work through the myriad issues that arise because they have different levels of religious observance has been given a rare and valuable opportunity to learn how to communicate. The members of this family have to talk to one another about issues that really matter, or they may cease being a family. They will have to work at creating family harmony instead of taking it for granted.

Every member of a family engaged in this struggle will learn about loving people for whom they are rather than for whom one wants them to be and about treating one another with respect and dignity, even if differing points of view make that difficult. Yes, conversation between me and my family members is difficult at times. But at least we are still talking, and we never give up on the vision we share of a loving, supportive, and connected family that spans three generations and a wide spectrum of religious practices.

If this book helps to create shalom bayis in even one family, it has been worth the effort. If it helps to build harmony and understanding within my own family, I will feel truly blessed beyond measure. To my parents' and siblings' credit, and to the credit of parents and siblings of newly observant Jews throughout the world, we are all learning how to be together as a family, despite the separateness we maintain in certain areas. It is not only possible, but it can be beautiful. We are all Jews, and we are family. We must never forget that.

WHAT DO YOU MEAN, YOU CAN'T EAT IN MY HOME?

One

WHAT DO YOU MEAN, YOU CAN'T EAT IN MY HOME?

How to Work Out Kashrus Issues

WHY IS FOOD SUCH A BIG DEAL?

So much of Judaism, both religious and secular, is focused around the kitchen table and the stomach that you may have heard the following joke:

> How can you sum up many Jewish holidays in four sentences?
>
> 1. They tried to kill us.
> 2. They failed.
> 3. We won.
> 4. Let's eat!

Name the Jewish holiday and the first thing that comes to mind is food. Chanukah—latkes; Rosh Hashanah—apples and honey; Pesach—matzoh brei; Purim—hamentashen; Shabbos—gefilte fish and kugel. Even some secular Jews refer to themselves with pride as "bagel and lox" Jews; they have shunned any form of religiosity, but they display their ethnic pride through what they consider one of the best parts of being a Jew—the food!

Food is often at the center of a family's life together, and anything that threatens a family's ability to eat together is seen as tearing apart the fabric of family life. Telling your mother you can't eat the food she has lovingly prepared for you in her kitchen may devastate the woman who has been feeding you from the day you were born.

It is estimated that only 10 percent of American Jews keep kosher today—all Orthodox Jews, some Conservative Jews, and a smaller percentage of Reform and Reconstructionist Jews. Even within that 10 percent, there are varying levels of kashrus observance in and out of the home. If your family's level of kashrus observance is not identical to yours and you don't take the time to prepare your family for your kashrus requirements, you will encounter dismay and confusion when you attempt to eat together.

Let's start by helping your family understand the philosophical underpinnings of keeping kosher. You will have to be able to explain to your family why you keep kosher and what keeping kosher actually entails. Your family may have only a cursory knowledge of kashrus and may hold some negative assumptions, which may lead to misunderstandings that can fuel unnecessary arguments. This can be especially tricky if your family does keep kosher, but not the same way that you do. So let's try to answer the first basic question.

WHY KEEP KOSHER? HOW SOME NONOBSERVANT JEWS VIEW KASHRUS

Many nonobservant Jews will acknowledge that, if they go back enough generations, they will come upon an ancestor who kept kosher. They will usually give one or more of the following explanations for why they do not believe it is necessary to continue this practice:

- Keeping kosher is no longer necessary or practical in modern-day, assimilated America.
- Keeping kosher separates observant Jews from nonobservant family members, friends, neighbors, and coworkers. It also makes them appear elitist, i.e., too good to eat the food of a decent fellow Jew or of anyone else with a clean kitchen and a good heart.
- The laws of kashrus were probably invented to protect Jews from unsanitary food preparation practices, but this is no longer necessary in today's highly regulated food-processing environment.
- Kosher food is expensive, and buying and preparing it is inconvenient. Keeping kosher unnecessarily limits what kinds of food can be consumed in a country where we are fortunate enough to enjoy a high standard of living and in a world where we have a bountiful variety of foods from which to choose.
- Keeping kosher makes it nearly impossible to go out to eat, unless you happen to live in an Orthodox Jewish neighborhood where there are kosher restaurants.

- Keeping kosher creates big headaches at family gatherings and celebrations, when the focus should be on enjoying oneself and not on worrying about whether the hot dogs are kosher.
- If God is the master of the universe, it doesn't make sense that He would care about whether a piece of cheese touches a hamburger.

During the course of a conversation about kashrus with nonobservant family members, you may hear some of the following:

- "What about respecting your parents and your family? Isn't that more important than keeping kosher?"
- "What could be nonkosher about a leaf of lettuce? Let's not get silly about this!"
- "My chicken-soup pot has only had chicken and vegetables in it! It's never even seen a pork chop!"
- "Will anything I do ever be good enough for you?"
- "Just because *you* want to keep kosher, does everyone else in the family have to be like you?"
- "I haven't been kosher a day in my life and God hasn't struck me down yet."
- "This is just the beginning. Next week you're going to grow side curls and a long beard and look like one of those Hasidim from Brooklyn."

You may also encounter family members of varying degrees of observance who feel that they do keep kosher. But their standards of kashrus are, for whatever reason, not the same as yours. In which case you may hear some of the following:

- "I've kept kosher longer than you've been alive!"
- "Uncle Harvey is kosher and he eats in our house!"
- "If it doesn't say 'pure vegetable oil' on the label, I won't bring it into the house. Why isn't that kosher enough for you?"

A good thing to keep in mind is that many family objections reflect the fear that you have made religion, including keeping kosher, more important than caring about your family. This is something you will want to address whenever you think it has become an issue for your family.

So, why *do* observant Jews keep the laws of kashrus? Here's one way of explaining it.

WHY KEEP KOSHER? HOW THE OBSERVANT JEW VIEWS KASHRUS

Although your relatives may believe that this is a very complex subject, and of course in some ways it is, here's the bottom-line answer to this question that really explains it best: "Because God told us to." For family members who want to understand more about this, we'll expand that thought with a bit more detail.

The observant Jew believes that Torah is the word of God, transmitted—at first directly, and then via Moses—by God to the Jewish people at Mount Sinai more than

3,300 years ago. If you believe in the divinity of God and in the revelation at Mount Sinai, you are obligated to follow the laws contained within the Torah for all eternity, as the Torah itself dictates.

Unless they are atheists or agnostics, most Jews believe that some sort of divine "being" or "essence" was responsible for creating the world. The primary difference between traditionally Torah-observant Jews and Jews who are not traditionally observant is in the degree to which each believes in the Torah as the blueprint for how you must (not "should" or "might want to") live your life.

If the Torah is the revealed word of God, and your goal in life is to live according to the way that God has outlined for you in His "book," everything contained in that book must be taken seriously—the parts that tell you to honor your parents and not commit adultery, and the parts that tell you which animals are okay to eat and which are not. Is it sometimes hard to understand exactly what the Torah is trying to say to us? Yes, of course. Must we then rely on people who are steeped in Torah knowledge to help us understand what the Torah means and how it applies to us in today's world? Yes, certainly. But this is the key point that is difficult for many nonobservant family members to understand: For the observant Jew, any debate on the importance of kashrus—or any other laws and precepts for that matter—is pointless. The only meaningful question is, "Did God give us the Torah?" If the absolute, undeniable answer to this question is "Yes!" then it is utterly logical for such a person to be completely committed to keeping kosher. It has absolutely nothing to do with how much you do or don't love the nonobservant members of your family.

ON A PERSONAL NOTE

Early on in my marriage to my husband Stephen (we've now been married for twelve years), when I begrudgingly agreed to keep a kosher home, I still ate nonkosher food outside of the home and fought like heck the concept that an all-knowing, all-powerful being could be watching to see whether or not a pork chop touched my lips—and if indeed He saw such a thing, that He would care. Having been on more than my share of diets over the years, this felt like just another diet that I was trying to keep for the sake of peace in my home.

For the purposes of family harmony, as I explained in detail in my book *Two Jews Can Still Be a Mixed Marriage*, Stephen and I settled on keeping an "almost" strictly kosher home, which meant that I sometimes purchased foods that did not have actual kosher certification as long as they did not contain any actual nonkosher ingredients. I learned about keeping separate sets of dishes for meat and dairy, keeping separate sets for Passover use, and keeping meat and dairy products separate. I purchased my meat only from a kosher butcher and my children were raised kosher from birth, so they never knew what a cheeseburger tasted like.

For a number of years I kept kosher for several reasons, none of them really having to do with "because God said so." Aside from accommodating my husband's wishes as to how he wanted our home to be run and our children to be educated, I viewed it as an opportunity to learn self-discipline (a practice I didn't always welcome). I loved the self-control I witnessed developing in my children. How many other children in a supermarket, having been told that a tempting piece of candy is "not kosher," would simply shrug and say, "Okay, Mama!" I found it compelling to infuse my day with a dose of Jewish identity every time I picked up a piece of food, first to say a blessing, and then with the understanding that what I was eating was in accordance with Jewish law.

After about four years I started feeling weird when I grabbed some French fries at Burger King. (I had long since given up eating nonkosher meat outside my home, but somehow I justified the French fries to myself as nothing but potatoes and oil.) But the main reason I stopped eating nonkosher outside my home was so that my three young children would receive a clear, consistent message about our family practice—we keep kosher, in and out of the house. Although I acted as if I believed that keeping kosher was important to God and I was at that time engaged in the study of Torah with rabbis and teachers, I was still keeping kosher only for the sake of my family. Although I would occasionally resent the restrictions, that was a good enough reason for me at that time in my life.

I will never forget the day that I lost all of my resistance to keeping strictly kosher. My husband and I, along with our children, were attending a weekend retreat sponsored by a Jewish outreach organization (Gateways) whose goal was a simple one: to convince everyone in attendance, regardless of their level of Jewish observance when they arrived, that it was God who wrote the Torah and that everything in it is as binding on us now as it was on the day it was given to the Children of Israel.

One lecture on kashrus changed my perspective forever. I would not be able to do it justice by paraphrasing it here. I'll just say that the rabbi thoroughly convinced me (and I'd say just about every person in the room) that it had to be God—and not assorted well-meaning human beings—who wrote the Torah and created the rules of kashrus. Once I believed this with both my heart and my mind, I could no longer eat in nonkosher restaurants or buy packaged food without kosher certification. All my former reasons for keeping kosher were still there, but they moved to the background. Along with my fellow observant Jews throughout history, I was finally able to feel (after six years of keeping kosher for other reasons) that I keep kosher because God wrote the Torah, and it says in the Torah that I must keep kosher.

Although I left the weekend retreat with a new commitment to kashrus and a more complete conviction that God was the One who came up with this idea of keeping kosher, a dissenting inner voice still nagged at me. What if all of this kashrus business was meant only for an earlier time in our history? Many Jews believe today that we must adjust our beliefs to new, more enlightened and welcoming surroundings. Can't the laws of kashrus be modified, even slightly, to accommodate a changing world?

If you, as a newly observant Jew, have never had this question run through your mind, I'd be surprised. I can practically guarantee that your family will raise it, if you haven't yourself. Here are some ways you might respond.

THE UNCHANGING TORAH

The short answer is, these laws can't be modified, even if we think they should be and even if we've justified to ourselves all kinds of important reasons for doing so. If your relatives would be interested in seeing some text from Torah that explains why, this passage from Deuteronomy 5:29 pretty much sums it up: "Be careful, then, to do as the Lord your God has commanded you. Do not turn aside to the right or to the left: Follow only the path that the Lord your God has enjoined upon you, so that you may thrive and that it may go well with you. . . ."

And then there's Deuteronomy 4:2. "You shall not add anything to what I command you or take anything away from it. . . ." These verses are traditionally interpreted to mean that the laws of kashrus (and all other laws in the Torah, for that matter) that were given to us thousands of years ago are as applicable today as they were then. There are laws we don't observe now because we literally can't—laws having to do with Temple rituals and laws applicable only to self-governing peoples, for example—but there's no getting out of observing the rest of them, including kashrus.

Your family will fight this concept; I certainly wrestled with it for a long time. Our culture is accustomed to evaluating time-honored practices and tossing out what is no longer relevant or what we now, in hindsight and/or after much soul-searching, feel was wrong or ill conceived. Jews who consider the Torah a well-intentioned guidebook to ethical and moral living feel free to do the same thing with everything contained within it. If it no longer makes "sense," we can dispense with it.

Observant Jews disagree. There are two types of laws in the Torah. *Mishpatim* are laws whose purpose is readily understandable in any civilized society—thou shalt not kill, thou shalt not steal, etc. *Chukim* are laws with no discernible practical reason—for example, you can't wear garments made of a mixture of linen and wool, and you can't eat any of the animals that are listed as prohibited in the Book of Leviticus.

If you believe that the Torah was written by some well-meaning men and women over the course of several hundred years to establish law and order over warrior tribes, of course you will choose to ignore the laws that don't seem necessary or applicable today. But if you believe that all these laws came from God, the fact that we don't understand the "why" behind some of them does not lessen our obligation to observe them. It just means that God chooses, in those instances, not to share His reasons for these laws with us. Do we know why God says it's okay to eat a veal chop but not a pork chop (as long as the veal was prepared according to the laws of kashrus)? No, we don't. Someday we may. But until we find out, we still can't eat the pork chop. Or I suppose we can, but we choose not to.

The secular Jew's goal is to adapt Jewish practices to allow him or her to function unimpeded in the world at large while still identifying as a Jew. Secular Jews have been astonishingly successful in achieving this goal, and they may rightfully balk at any approach to life that would undermine this accomplishment. Here's one of the defining differences between an observant Jew and a nonobservant Jew: *The observant Jew's goal is to adapt himself to fit the laws of Torah, never to adapt the Torah to fit his ways of doing things.* Even though performing some mitzvos, such as doing acts of kindness for others, might make us "feel good," that is never seen as the primary reason for doing them. If that were the case, we would feel justified in discarding the mitzvos that no longer make us "feel good." And that is something observant Jews would never do.

During my first few years of keeping kosher, I approached the laws of kashrus as if they were mishpatim. I searched for the reasons, and when they made sense to me, I complied. I was very surprised to discover that keeping kosher falls in the category of chukim—laws given to us by God for reasons only God knows. We may assume we know some of the reasons God wants Jews to keep kosher, and we may believe that we understand the wisdom of these laws and what they are meant to accomplish. But the fact is, we really don't know and we keep kosher, anyway. Why? Because God tells us to!

BUT WHERE IN THE BIBLE DOES IT SAY YOU CAN'T EAT A CHEESEBURGER?

It doesn't, of course. And that could be the first argument put forth by a family member who has no problem with keeping what some call "biblical kosher"—following what they believe is clearly written in the Torah. They don't eat shellfish, but they feel perfectly comfortable eating a cheeseburger because nowhere in the written Torah does it say not to eat meat and dairy together. How do you explain the Oral Law to your family? It's not easy, but here's a head start.

Observant Jews believe that along with the Torah, which was written down by Moses, God also explained passages that were purposely left ambiguous in the text, as well as provided additional laws, some of which can be derived from the text and some of which are not derivable from the text. These thousands of laws were meant to be transmitted orally from generation to generation. These laws eventually did get written down, in the Mishnah, which was completed in the third century of the Common Era. Rabbinic discussions about the interpretation and meaning of these laws were set down in the Talmud, which was completed in the sixth century of the Common Era. Since that time, various codes of Jewish law have been compiled by rabbinic leaders of subsequent eras. They contain elucidations of the Oral Law as it applies to modern times and modern innovations. It's the Oral Law that tells us we can't eat a cheeseburger. Here's the part that will be the hardest for your family to understand (and often, the hardest leap for the newly observant Jew to make as well!): *For observant Jews, the laws of the Mishnah and Talmud are as binding as the laws in the Torah.* They represent God's commentary on His Torah. Less observant Jews believe these texts are interesting but nonbinding commentary. Torah-observant Jews believe that they are divinely ordained laws that must be followed precisely as written.

Jews who strictly adhere to the laws of kashrus despite pressures to be "more flexible" are demonstrating a commitment, first and foremost, to obey God as master and creator of the universe. If anyone, in the hopes of persuading you to drop or modify the practice, suggests to you that keeping kosher doesn't make sense, they will be disappointed. You can vigorously agree: "You're right. Keeping kosher makes no sense. But God must have a good reason for requiring it. Since I have no way of discerning fully what that reason is, I must put my faith in God and do it anyway."

To the observant Jew, the question "Does God care whether I eat a cheeseburger?" is no different than questioning whether God cares about any of the other mitzvos that are in the Torah, the Mishnah, the Talmud, or any of the codes of Jewish law. It isn't subject to debate. Of course God cares, or God wouldn't have set down these laws.

OKAY, I GET IT. BUT WHY DOES MY SON (OR DAUGHTER) HAVE TO BE SO OBNOXIOUS ABOUT IT?

What's the big deal about eating a single slice of nonkosher cheese, or enjoying an occasional cookie that comes out of a package that isn't marked "kosher"? You might be able to help your family understand why you can't eat a cheeseburger, but they may still wonder, Do you have to be so rigid about every little thing that enters your mouth? Well, yes, you do. You believe that, in addition to violating Jewish law by eating nonkosher food, there are serious spiritual consequences from doing so, that consuming nonkosher food is bad for your soul. Ultimately, just as your parents aim to "do good," by cooking a scrumptious meal or picking up the tab for a delicious meal at a restaurant, you also want to do good—in the eyes of God. But sometimes, in your zeal to please God, you may act in ways that offend your family, especially if your approach is what some would term "obnoxious."

Let's assume that all the members of your family have come to understand your position on kashrus, even if they don't agree with it. Even in these ideal circumstances, you'll still hear family members muttering to themselves, or even directly to you, "This couldn't be what God had in mind—creating so much family trouble over food!" On this we can all agree. No one relishes the family strife that comes from working out kashrus issues.

Sometimes the problem lies not in what you are asking of your family, but in how you approach the whole subject in the first place. Unfortunately, the parent who is fed up with dealing with the "rigid, opinionated, observant son or daughter who thinks he or she is better than everyone else" fails to see the beauty in the practice that causes this tension.

Some newly observant Jews develop the well-meaning but unpopular habit of trying to convince family members to become kosher themselves, to the point where being around them, especially at mealtimes, becomes intolerable. Don't bring it up at every opportunity, or flaunt your observance of kashrus as a spiritual yardstick for being a better Jew. When your sister is enthusiastically digging into her bacon and eggs at breakfast, don't glare at her with a look that says "You are disgusting to me!" It will not make her put down her fork and surrender her plate to you. It only intensifies the power struggle. If you do secretly hope that one day your family will eat only kosher, not only will these actions damage that possibility, they will also make your family less likely to want to accommodate your kashrus requirements.

It's normal to want to share something that's important to you with the people whom you love. But your enthusiasm can be misinterpreted as coercion, particularly when you are trying to convince someone who you think is doing something wrong to radically change his lifestyle and do it the "right" way. Yes, you are doing it for noble motives, but you have to look at what you are doing from your family's point of view. Your mother, for example, might be thinking something like this: "My daughter keeps trying to convince me to keep kosher because she thinks the way I've lived my life for the past sixty years is wrong and she, of course, knows better than I do about what's right and wrong!" Well, if that is how she feels, no wonder she thinks you're being obnoxious! But I believe it's shortsighted to think that this is the sole motivation behind your overeager, and, yes, sometimes quite annoying refusal to give up on trying to get your family to keep kosher. See if this also rings true for you: Most people, no matter how old they are, crave their parents' respect and approval. If you can get your family to take on the religious obligations that you have assumed, even if only to some extent, that's one way for you to know that your family approves of you.

If you can communicate this to your family, perhaps they will understand that, even with all the spiritual sustenance you receive from observing the Torah and from being a part of your observant community, what you really crave is hearing your parents say something like, "I'm really impressed with the way you stick with your commitments, and I'm proud of you. I don't want to stop making my chicken soup for you. I know how much you love it, and I love cooking for you. Can you show me how to make my soup for you so you can eat it?"

ON A PERSONAL NOTE

Even as I write these words, tears come to my eyes. In my family we have achieved a truce after twelve years of my keeping a kosher home and their not doing so. Harsh words are rare, and we are becoming more accustomed to working out the details required for getting together. This usually means that Stephen and I bring our own food to family get-togethers and look away from what anyone else is eating. Most times, we serve as the hosts so that we can supply the food for everyone. But, still, the little girl in me longs for something I have never gotten from my family, from my parents in particular: a genuine, heartfelt expression from them that my Jewish observance makes them proud—that they think that I have "done good."

I regret that my religious observance is a source of embarrassment, and not pride, to my family. It's a feeling that, thankfully, they have learned to keep to themselves, but it leaks out every now and then. It pains me to know that my parents can't be as proud of me, or of their grandchildren, as I have always longed for them to be. I am in my mid-forties as I write this. The longing for parental approval does not disappear with age. Perhaps it diminishes in time as you make peace with its absence, but it never goes away entirely.

TO SUM IT UP—A MORE POSITIVE APPROACH

Here's a rule of thumb that applies to every subject we'll cover in this book: *A loving approach that communicates the value you place on your family and on your relationship with them works a whole lot better than lecturing.*

The parent or other family member who appears belligerent and unwilling to accommodate you to the slightest degree hopes to hear from you something like this: "I need you to work with me, because I don't want to go through life not being able to eat your delicious food or to join you at your table. I love you, and I want to remain close to you, regardless of our differences in religious practice."

PRACTICAL ISSUES REGARDING KEEPING KOSHER WHEN YOUR FAMILY DOESN'T

While I was growing up, I didn't know a single Jew who kept kosher. But somehow I picked up the most cursory understanding of kosher practices: no shellfish, no pork, no cheeseburgers.

It was actually a great surprise to me, as an adult learning the laws of kashrus, to discover that keeping kosher is much more involved than that. Kashrus can be broken down into three categories—what foods you can and can't eat, how food is processed, and how it is cooked. Why go through all this in such detail here? Why isn't it sufficient to say to your family something like, "Listen, if you aren't going to keep kosher, you don't need to know all this. Just trust me, there are a lot of rules that I have to pay attention to, so just do what I tell you to do."

I hope in this chapter to show you how to diffuse tensions that may arise from a superficial understanding of kashrus. If your family believes that keeping kosher only means avoiding shellfish, pork, and cheeseburgers, then it will be hurtful to them when you refuse to eat the egg-salad sandwich your mom prepared in her kitchen. Likewise, you will be able to avoid offending your sister-in-law, who has just gone to considerable effort to make you matzoh-ball soup in the same pot in which she also made cream of mushroom soup for your dad, if you can explain to her that dairy and meat products can't be cooked in the same pot.

If you've been keeping kosher for a long time, you are probably familiar with the basics of kashrus practice. What follows is a summary, something you can either give your relatives to read or simply review on your own so that you can recall the relevant details when the topic of kashrus comes up with your family. And who knows, you might even learn something you didn't already know. I did, when researching the laws in the course of writing this book!

Prohibited Foods

Why is shellfish—such as lobster, shrimp, crab, and clams, for example—prohibited? Because, according to the Bible, only fish that have both fins and scales are kosher. That's also why fish such as swordfish and catfish are not kosher. For an observant Jew to be able to consume fish purchased in a store, there must be evidence that the fish had scales (sometimes there is a tag on the skinned fish that indicates this), and the consumer must know that the fish did not come into contact with the oil from a nonkosher fish (through the use of a common knife and/or cutting board).

Your relatives are probably familiar with the "no lobster" rule, but it will probably come as a big surprise to them that they can't just pick up a few pounds of fresh, filleted salmon at their local supermarket without dealing with kashrus issues.

When I was living in an area where the nearest kosher fish store was an hour away, I would sometimes buy a whole fish at the fish market and have my husband filet it at home (a messy, time-consuming ordeal). Many members of my Orthodox community would bring their own knives and wax paper (for the scale) to the supermarket and ask the fellow behind the counter to cut up and filet a whole fish and weigh it using the kosher supplies they provided.

Why is pork prohibited? Because, according to the Bible, kosher animals must chew their cud and have split hooves. A rabbit chews its cud, but doesn't have split hooves. A pig has split hooves but doesn't chew its cud. A cow does both. So do a lamb and a deer. But they must be slaughtered by a certified shochet, or slaughterer, in accordance with Jewish law. Blood and certain parts of the animal must be removed, again in accordance with Jewish law. And the meat must be prepared using only pots, grills, utensils, etc., that have not been used to prepare nonkosher food or dairy products. That's why, if Uncle Joe shoots a deer in the woods, even though deer is a kosher animal, you can't eat it because it wasn't killed, prepared, and cooked according to Jewish law.

The Bible lists certain fowl that are not kosher—eagles and swans, for example—but chicken, turkey, duck, and goose are kosher, as long as they are slaughtered and prepared according to Jewish law.

No form of insect is deemed kosher for eating today. "No problem," you might say. "I wouldn't want to eat a spider or a cockroach anyway!" This is a more serious issue for observant Jews than it appears. In recent years the use of certain pesticides became prohibited by law. Since then, much of our produce, unless grown hydroponically, has become infested with tiny, hard-to-see insects that must be thoroughly washed away under running water before the food is eaten. (There's one advantage to keeping kosher—your relatives can be assured that any salad they eat in your home is really, really clean!) Cleaning vegetables may sound simple, but think about broccoli florets, with all those hard-to-reach places for those tiny bugs to hang out. You can see why many observant Jews—and the rest of the public as well—are snatching up bags of prewashed vegetables that can be found in supermarkets that are located in neighborhoods with large observant Jewish populations. If you want to make it easy on your relatives when it comes to the salad, show them how to look in the supermarket for salad bags that come with kosher certification. It makes life easier for everyone, especially the host!

Are there any prohibitions on purchasing or eating fruit and vegetables? There is a whole set of rules regarding the purchase of produce grown in Israel, but it won't come up often in your family so we'll skip that level of detail. Consult your rabbi for more information on this.

Processed Foods and Kosher Certification

Processed and precooked food must be prepared under rabbinical supervision, and food prepared under such supervision will carry on its packaging a symbol that indicates which kosher certification agency was used. This certification means that the food started off kosher and did not come into contact with anything not kosher (i.e., other food products, utensils, or equipment used to prepare nonkosher food) during the entire process of preparation.

Most American Jews are familiar with the Ⓤ symbol of the Orthodox Union, and so it comes as a surprise to many that there are actually hundreds of kosher certifying agencies in the United States. Some employ many rabbinical supervisors and monitor multitudes of manufacturers. Some are one- or two-person operations that monitor only a few companies. Unfortunately, there is no religious body through which all of these agencies can be licensed. The larger ones are affiliated with rabbinical organizations with impeccable international reputations. Some of the smaller ones may be run by rabbis who are highly regarded within their local communities. But the short of it is, not all kashrus agencies and symbols are created equal, and observant Jews will be very careful about which kashrus agencies they consider reliable and which they do not.

You will have to explain all this to your family, because a package of food that has an artistically rendered kashrus symbol on it does not necessarily mean that you will eat the food inside of it. The "K" that appears on some packages is particularly problematic. "But the 'K' means kosher, right?" your mom might say. Not necessarily. Because the letter "K" is a letter of the alphabet, it cannot be copyrighted, and it may be placed on a package by the manufacturer even if there was no rabbinical supervision. Observant Jews won't eat packaged food unless they can determine under whose rabbinical supervision it was produced.

If your family mistakenly believes that the ® on the package, which stands for registered trademark, is a kosher symbol, don't make them feel stupid for making an honest mistake. Many observant Jews have trouble keeping track of all the kosher designations out there nowadays!

Most kashrus-observing Jews will eat anything that carries the symbols of one of the major kosher-certifying agencies: Ⓤ, כK, Ⓚ, or ☆K. There are, however, observant Jews who, as regards dairy products, assume additional stringencies: They will eat only those dairy products whose production has been supervised by observant Jews from the milking of the cow to the final packaging. Dairy products prepared this way are called Cholov Yisroel, and would be designated as such on the package.

If your family is not happy about your level of religious observance to begin with, the extra effort expended to buy food that you will be able to eat might make them even more resentful. They may say directly to you (or they may comment to another family member, who then passes it on to you) something like, "Why can't I put our favorite family salad dressing on the salad? It's just oil and a bunch of spices!" Or, "This is ridiculous, paying twice the price for kosher cheese and meat. It's all the same food, anyway. They won't even know the difference if I just throw the wrappers away!"

The requirements of kashrus are considerable, and for someone who doesn't believe in them in the first place, spending time and energy fulfilling these requirements might well bring on an emotional response. All you can do is offer to help your family as much as possible, offering to buy all the food yourself, or to go shopping for it together with them. Many newly observant Jews choose simply to bring their own food to family gatherings, which makes it easier on everyone. Always express your sincere gratitude for the trouble and inconvenience your family is going through on your behalf. And remember that most of your family's resentment is coming from two emotions: confusion about getting it all right, and fear that they will do something "wrong." My purpose for writing this book is to help you and your family deal with these feelings in a constructive way.

HOW TO PREPARE, COOK, AND EAT KOSHER FOOD IN A NONKOSHER KITCHEN

Yes, the easiest way to deal with this issue is by sliding a big cooler into the trunk of your car and bringing your own food. But that option doesn't work so well if you're traveling by airplane (although some kashrus-observing Jews will cook, seal, and freeze their food and then bring the frozen meals, packed in ice, along with them on the airplane; it can be done!). And what do you do if your mom says to you, "Just tell me what to buy and what I need to do to my kitchen so that you can eat with all of us. If I buy Empire chicken instead of Perdue, will that do the trick?"

Such an invitation is a real act of love and an effort to bridge the gap between you and your family. Avoid the impulse to reflexively say, "Forget it, Mom, it's too complicated. We'll just bring our own food and paper plates," because you will hurt her feelings and destroy any possibility of your family accepting with love and understanding your decision to become observant. It comes as a surprise to many newly observant Jews that, under certain circumstances, you can eat kosher food that has been prepared in a nonkosher kitchen. (That said, if your family is so angry about your observance that you feel all efforts to prepare your kosher food will be undermined, either directly or subtly, if they are involved in food preparation, you might have to gently explain that you prefer to bring your own food, although you appreciate their offer.)

If you do want to make the effort to cook food in your family's nonkosher kitchen, where do you start? *Remember, it's not the house that is or is not kosher, it's the food and how it is prepared.* We'll start off with the shopping. Buying packaged foods is easy. Describe the types of kosher certification seals they will need to look for on food packages (the easiest ones to identify are the ones listed on page 25), and remember to mention that no dairy products (which will be designated on packaged food with a "D" or "Dairy" next to the kashrus symbol) can be served at a meat meal or for three to six hours after that meat meal (the number of hours depends on your own personal practice). Parve food, which is neither meat nor dairy—fish, eggs, fruit, vegetables, beans, nuts, and grain products—can be eaten together with either meat or dairy products, so long as they did not themselves become dairy or meat by being prepared in dairy or meat pots.

You'll have to plan the menu together with your family. The person doing the cooking probably doesn't know that not only can't she make beef Stroganoff with sour cream for you, but that you can't enjoy her famous dairy chocolate cake—the family favorite—if it follows a meat meal (and, of course, if it was baked in nonkosher pans, in a nonkosher oven, but we'll get to that in a bit).

So what do you tell the host who thinks that substituting kosher chicken for nonkosher chicken takes care of the chicken problem? Or what if she is generous enough to say, "There's a kosher butcher shop right here in town, so I'll buy all the meat from them." Given the extra expense of that decision, the offer deserves a big hug! Now you'll have to explain: "Just as there isn't one standard kosher certification for packaged food, there isn't one, universally accepted, government-regulated standard for what is sold in a butcher shop that puts a KOSHER sign in its window. I'll need the phone number of the shop so I can ask the propietor a few questions before I can tell you if I can eat their meat." Once you've determined that the local butcher has appropriate rabbinic supervision according to your personal standards, and you've explained to your family that when they buy the chicken (which has been packaged to indicate that it comes from a kosher source), they can put it into their own refrigerator as long as it is completely wrapped, we're headed in the right direction.

Now let's figure out how to cook or grill that bird. Here

comes another delicate issue. Your family was considerate enough to buy new pots, pans, and utensils (which you will have to immerse in a mikvah before they are used), or they have stored in a cabinet the things they bought specially for you, for when you visit. Or, you've agreed to use those disposable aluminum pans that you can easily find, in any size you need, in the supermarket. Now you need to convey the fact that you must be around to watch the food preparation. The person doing the cooking could easily be offended. "I know how to cook!" she may say. "You don't trust me?" It's so hard to say so, but no, you don't, not when it comes to following the laws of kashrus. It's not your family's fault, it's just that you are so much more familiar with the rules than they are, and you have much more at stake in making sure the details are taken care of. You can't expect your family to be as stringent as you would be. Turn this into an opportunity for the kind of time together that is hard to find in busy adult lives. Consider it "schmoozing" time, rather than "supervising" time.

If the chicken is kosher and so is the pot, does the fork really matter that much? You'll have to explain: Utensils also affect the kashrus of the food being prepared. Pots and utensils (such as mixing and serving spoons) that were used to prepare nonkosher food may be so spotless and clean that you can see your reflection in them, but because they came into contact with hot and/or liquid nonkosher food, they are considered to have absorbed nonkosher essence and taste, and therefore have also become nonkosher. By drinking water that had been boiled in a clean pot, a great chef can tell you what had previously been cooked in that pot. Even though the average palate can't tell that the pot that just cooked your beef stew for dinner was used to prepare corn chowder with milk for lunch, the laws of kashrus are sensitive to this issue. A cook who doesn't understand why one fork could be considered a meat utensil and another fork a dairy utensil could easily mix the two up in the process of food preparation. That's another reason you need to be in the kitchen while the cooking is going on.

Aside from the issue of mixing meat and dairy, there's also the risk of the kosher food coming into contact with nonkosher food already in the home. If the person doing the cooking buys kosher steak but then mistakenly puts nonkosher steak sauce on it, the meat is considered nonkosher. It could even be much more accidental than that. Although all salt and nonprocessed spices are kosher, many processed spices are not kosher. The well-meaning grandmother who puts the kosher roast into a new kosher pot but then sprinkles it liberally with a plethora of nonkosher spices because she doesn't realize that spices must be kosher certified will unwittingly make the entire roast off-limits to you. Imagine how terrible you'll feel telling her that, after she went through such trouble and expense to accommodate you!

If you decide to eat kosher food prepared in a nonkosher kitchen, you will first have to focus on three basic things: (1) all food purchased must carry acceptable kosher certification, and the packages must remain sealed until you open them; (2) all new or kashered cooking utensils, pots, and pans must be designated for use with either dairy or meat products, and you will have to supervise the preparation of the food in them; (3) your meals will have to be eaten on either paper plates or on dishes designated as either meat or dairy. But we're getting ahead of ourselves. Let's go back to the food preparation stage, now that you've explained to your family why you must be part of this process. How do you make your family's oven or barbecue kosher?

Kashering the Oven, Pots, and Utensils

Even if the oven has been regularly used to cook nonkosher foods, don't worry, it's fairly easy to kasher an oven. Turn a self-cleaning oven on to the two-hour, short cycle or turn any oven on to "broil" for one hour and all the nonkosher taste and residual food will have been burned away. An oven that is not self-cleaning needs to be treated with a caustic cleaner, such as Easy-Off—sometimes twice—before you turn it on and do the burning out. Different types of stovetops have different kashering requirements. Consult your rabbi for this. If there isn't a designated set of kosher pots that your family stores away for your visits and they don't go for the idea of using disposable aluminum pans, you could ask your rabbi about kashering some of your family's pots, pans, and utensils, but this is a complicated procedure and might annoy everyone. I'd suggest staying away from that alternative. Nowadays it's easy to purchase the inexpensive utensils you'll need for a short visit, and then you'll have them for the next time you come for a visit. Just store them in a place where they can't get mixed up with the nonkosher utensils. Doing this will reassure your family that you plan to come back again!

There is one suggestion I can offer you from the five months Stephen and I spent living in our attic with our kids while our house was gutted and transformed from a two-family home into a one-family. We didn't have a kitchen in the attic, so we made do mostly with a meat crockpot, a dairy crockpot, a George Foreman minigrill, and a toaster oven. It's amazing how easy it is to prepare a whole meal in one crockpot! You can purchase all of these items fairly inexpensively nowadays, so if there is one family home in particular that you plan to visit often, you might consider buying and storing some or all of these items there. Or, for your next birthday, suggest to your folks that they buy for you a few of these appliances to keep at their home for when you visit.

Now on to the outdoor grill. It's possible to kasher a grill by cleaning all the grates and burying them in white-hot coals for fifteen minutes before grilling the food, but your family will probably not be enthusiastic about using that much charcoal (although they may love an excuse to get their grill sparkling clean!). It would be better to keep a designated kosher grill at your family's home, or you can buy a disposable grill in the supermarket. Most indoor ovens now offer the option of cooking on the stovetop with a grill pan.

If your mom insists on kashering an existing pot rather than buying a new one for you, you'll have to make sure that the pot has not been used for twenty-four hours before you arrive to do the actual kashering. Only then can the pot be kashered. Silverware is kashered by boiling it briefly in a kosher pot of water. Consult your rabbi for the details on both of these procedures. I still think it's a better idea to pick up an inexpensive set of pots and utensils that you can use for kosher cooking.

Now let's say that you are satisfied that the ingredients of the meal are kosher; the pots, pans, and cooking utensils are kosher; and the end result will be a kosher meal that you can enjoy. How do you eat this food on Mom's non-kosher china if she's really put off by your using paper plates?

EATING KOSHER FOOD ON NONKOSHER PLATES, AND OTHER MISCELLANEOUS ISSUES

You may often try to make life simpler for all concerned by eating everything on paper plates, but you may be unnecessarily separating yourself from your family or calling attention to your kashrus practices when you don't need to be doing so. Imagine how your mom will feel when she has put so much effort into preparing the meal so it will be kosher, but then you refuse to eat on regular dishes like everyone else? It can be hurtful.

If you will be eating often in this home, purchase some extra plates and silverware (both meat and dairy) for your use, and store them carefully away. Don't forget that you will need to *toivel* (ritually immerse) them. You may even be able to match or come close to the patterns on the china and silverware that everyone else will be using. It's also a good idea to buy designated cutting boards for meat and dairy—again, easily picked up for a few dollars at the local supermarket or dollar store—and separate carving knives for meat and dairy that you can bring with you (or purchase there if you'll be traveling by plane). If it's a special occasion, and it's important to Mom or Grandma that everyone use the fine china that has sentimental family value attached to it, with a little effort on your part you may be able to use these dishes, too.

As long as the food is not hot (i.e., it's served cold or at room temperature), you can eat your kosher food on plates that have been used to serve nonkosher food. This is not an ideal solution, but it can be done on an occasional basis, if there is no other option. If a hot meal is being served, you won't be able to use those nonkosher dishes. But if cold tuna salad and bagels are on the menu, you can enjoy the meal on Mom's dishes without worrying. And here's a novel idea that someone told me she's done: If the food is hot, put clear glass plates (that are themselves kosher, of course) on top of the family china and put your food on the glass plates. Maybe that seems like too much trouble, but if it's important to your host that your dishes not clash with her beautiful table settings, your effort to blend in with the rest of the family will be appreciated.

Your family will be happy to hear that it's not necessary to kasher their refrigerator, because all of the food in it is cold. You must be sure, however, that any kosher food does not come in contact with nonkosher food in the refrigerator. Tupperware and zip-locked plastic bags are particularly good for storing leftovers that you'll want to take home with you.

So, there you have it—you can enjoy a kosher brisket prepared in Mom's nonkosher kitchen. And if she's willing to substitute nondairy, soy-based cream for sour cream, you can even have her beef Stroganoff. Now let's tackle one more sensitive issue that will come up when you eat with your family.

BLESSINGS AND HAND-WASHING

The food is kosher, you've worked out the dishes issue, and then you come to an awkward moment. The family is digging into the basket of rolls on the table and your kids look at you with horrified expressions. "Mommy, they didn't wash before eating the bread!" You will have to remember to discuss this issue with your children before the visit, to explain to them that your relatives do not share your immediate family's commitment to saying blessings before eating and to performing the ritual hand-washing if bread is being served. However you choose to explain your relatives' nonobservance to your children, you will want to avoid public condemnation of nonobservant behavior.

If you are eating a Shabbos meal with your relatives in their home, hopefully they will accommodate your desire to say the blessings over the wine and bread that are part of the Sabbath ritual—even if they just sit silently and look down at their napkins. Speak to your hosts ahead of time and let them know about your need to say these important prayers. If they are really resistant to your inviting everyone to participate, then don't do so. But this should not affect what you yourself do; never skip these prayers just to keep peace. Just say them with your own immediate family.

As regards how this affects your children, in my experience, if you don't make a big deal out of your relatives' nonobservance, your children won't, either. It simply becomes something they are used to. "Aunt Jackie and my cousins don't keep kosher, and that's just the way it is in our family."

TO SUM IT ALL UP

It is possible to eat a kosher meal in a nonkosher home. It takes a bit of extra time, some extra effort, and some preplanning, but it is doable. Is it the ideal way to eat kosher food? Of course not. But if it's important to you and your family to share some time together and if this can't be done in your own home, what I've explained above will allow you to do so. It will also demonstrate to your family that, even though your religious practices are different from theirs, this doesn't mean you don't care about them. When you can, host family gatherings in your own home. When that's not possible, take the time to explain to your relatives why you are doing what you are doing, and what you'll need if you are going to eat in their home. And always do it with love.

WHAT ABOUT EATING IN RESTAURANTS?

What's wrong with joining us for a tuna sandwich? Isn't tuna kosher?

Ah, I wish it were that simple. A common misconception is that an observant Jew can eat a salad or any cold "kosher" food served in any restaurant, kosher or not. Many

Jews who consider themselves kashrus-observant elect to do this, which makes this topic very confusing to discuss with your family. Alas, a nonkosher restaurant is no different than Mom's nonkosher kitchen. The tuna needs to come from a can with a kosher symbol on it; the mayonnaise needs to be kosher, and so does the bread. The lettuce has to be checked for bugs. The tomato must be sliced with a kosher knife, and the tuna and mayo must be scooped out with kosher utensils and mixed in a kosher bowl. Not so simple, is it?

If the option of ordering a plate of whole fruit and cutting it with a knife you bring along doesn't appeal to you (it won't appeal to most people), and if you don't want to bring along your own food (according to Jewish law, an observant Jew should avoid being seen entering a nonkosher restaurant so that other observant Jews won't mistakenly assume either that the food served there is kosher or that he is intentionally violating Jewish law by eating in a nonkosher restaurant), the easiest solution is for everyone to eat at a kosher restaurant if there is one within a reasonable driving distance.

If your family agrees to eat with you at a kosher restaurant, remember that this represents a big concession on their part and you shouldn't take it for granted. Because kashrus is so important to you, it's easy to forget that your family is doing this just to accommodate you; they would most likely prefer to eat elsewhere. If this decision will result in extra expense for everyone, you might offer to pick up the tab, to pay more than your share, or to take care of the tip. If there is no kosher restaurant within a reasonable driving distance, you can offer to meet up with everyone after dinner, or to host everyone at your home. If there are young children involved, your family might be happy to eat in your home and not have to worry about how the children are behaving in a restaurant.

If none of the above will work and your family picks a nonkosher restaurant that has a bar as well as table seating, you can enter the establishment. (Because the bar presents the option of simply having a soda, you don't have to worry about observant Jews mistakenly assuming you are entering the restaurant to eat.) You can have a soda while your family eats, and while the sight of a cheeseburger or some of the other nonkosher food might make you feel uncomfortable, skip the grimaces. You aren't spending time with your family because of the meal, but, rather, for the experience of being together with them. Reassure your mom that you ate before you came, so you aren't hungry.

The newly observant Jew who says to family members, "If you don't keep kosher, I can't eat with you!" is mistaken. And the family members who say "We aren't going to put up with your craziness. If you want to eat with us, you'll eat what we eat, or forget about it!" are taking a situation where compromise is possible and turning it into a source of tension and pain. In both instances everyone is missing out on a huge opportunity to express the love that they feel for one another. When both you and your family go the extra mile to show that you value the relationships you have with one another, you will see how much progress you will make in reaching the point where your relatives understand and accept your new way of life. Breakthroughs such as these are not only possible, but likely.

ON A PERSONAL NOTE

I have been blessed in my life with a special relationship with my great-aunt, Edith, who recently passed away. She was my mother's aunt through marriage—not even a blood relative of mine—and yet she was the closest I've ever come to having a grandparent. Two out of my four grandparents died before I was born. The other two died when I was young, and I scarcely knew them. But Aunt Edith never missed a family simchah, and no matter how she aged, she always impressed me with her elegance, grace, and gentleness. She is the only elderly relative in all of the family photos, and the only family member from her generation whom I knew. I had great respect for her.

A couple of years ago Aunt Edith relocated from her New York City apartment to an independent living facility an hour's drive from my home in Highland Park, New Jersey. This gave me the unique opportunity to visit her regularly with my children. Ironically, although the issues of eating or not eating with my parents and siblings are far more complicated than anything I'd experienced with Aunt Edith, it was on my visits with her that I felt most acutely the core issues that I've discussed in this chapter.

On the day we came, I imagine that Aunt Edith spent a good deal of time preparing for our visit. To me, she still looked as beautiful as she did twenty years earlier, her silver hair elegantly coiffed, her appearance immaculate. When we visited, we'd knock and then enter her apartment, and we always found her sitting regally in her chair, awaiting us, dressed in her finest. She smiled in delight at the sight of my beautiful young children, and they lovingly and dutifully gave her a kiss on the cheek. And always laid out on her coffee table was a lovely arrangement of cookies, removed from their wrappers and beautifully placed, beckoning to my children, whose eyes lit up upon seeing them.

The first time this happened, I recognized the brand and silently thanked God that they were kosher, but I also knew they that were dairy. And that was a problem. I had just taken the children to eat at a kosher hamburger joint near my aunt's apartment. I'd like to tell those of you testing my firm commitment to Yiddishkeit that I immediately yanked the cookies out of my children's hands. Truthfully (and I will be truthful about my own dilemmas throughout this book), I did absolutely nothing when my aunt handed the cookies to my children and each shyly took one. I froze. There was my dear, quite elderly Aunt Edith, who had gone through so much trouble to prepare this treat for my children, and I didn't have the heart, or the stomach, to ruin the scene. I didn't plan to eat the cookies myself, but I was going to allow my children to enjoy them. But then my oldest daughter, who was seven at the time, asked me halfway through her first cookie, "Mommy, are these cookies kosher? Mommy, are these parve? We just ate meat!" So I had to deal with it after all.

Why was this moment so hard for me? Working out kashrus with my parents and siblings has been a much greater challenge in terms of all the details involved, but this moment with Aunt Edith best exemplifies for me the quandary of being an observant Jew in a nonobservant family. I couldn't fathom any way, down to the fiber of my being, that I could hurt sweet Aunt Edith's feelings. I held her in high esteem and gave her the respect due the oldest living relative in my family. I couldn't embarrass her, distress her, or upset her in any way. And yet my children were depending on me to lead them on the right course, to help them make kashrus decisions for them, until they were old enough to make those decisions for themselves. I felt trapped in a no-win situation. I knew that the right thing to do would be to tell my children that they couldn't eat the cookies because they were dairy and to try to explain it to Aunt Edith. But I didn't. My oldest daughter, who knew better, stopped eating her cookie when I wouldn't give her a straight answer about whether or not the cookies were parve. My other two were too young to understand the issues. Now all three are old enough—and knowledgeable enough about kashrus—that I couldn't get away with this.

Every time we visited Aunt Edith, the same brand of cookies was on the table, so we tried to organize our visits so that we were not coming directly from a meat meal. From time to time, I would bring my own pots and kosher mac-and-cheese to cook in my aunt's apartment, or I would shlep along a box of kosher pizza and wrap the slices in aluminum foil to be heated in my aunt's oven. I often apologized for not joining her for lunch in the facility's dining room. It was always with a twinge of regret that I did so, because I saw the sadness in her eyes when she asked in her soft, nondemanding voice, "Can't you just join me for a tuna sandwich in the dining room, dear?"

Ah, I wish I could have. And that's the point. I *do* wish I could have. But I couldn't, and neither could my children, because keeping kosher is not a practice that we can, or will, suspend when it becomes inconvenient or uncomfortable. These dilemmas are not easy, but they *can* be worked through. The bottom line is that I didn't allow kashrus concerns to stop me or my children from visiting Aunt Edith. And that's what really matters.

Two

WHAT DO YOU MEAN, YOU CAN'T ANSWER THE PHONE FOR TWO DAYS?

How to Explain Sabbath and Jewish Holiday Observances

Weekends and holidays are traditionally times when families get together. There is no denying the beauty of seeing three generations of a family assembled for the holidays. For families that have moved apart geographically, it's particularly important to have these opportunities to reconnect, to rekindle the closeness that adult siblings might have shared when they were younger, and to bring together grandparents and their beloved grandchildren. When a family member becomes observant, the fear is that these special times will be lost.

The Torah and the voluminous codes of Jewish law provide fairly straightforward answers to questions about religious practice, ritual, and observance, but many of the questions that will arise when you spend Shabbos and Jewish holidays with your family are more sociological and psychological than legalistic.

The first thing we'll do is clarify what the religious obligations are for observing Shabbos and the holidays, and then we'll discuss the best ways to handle the most common problems you'll encounter when you spend these times with family—and what to do when you elect not to do so.

CAN'T WE JUST AVOID THE WHOLE ISSUE?

Given the choice of dealing with these issues head-on or avoiding them entirely, avoidance is definitely the simpler option. Some families—and this includes my own—choose to avoid family visits that involve any religious holiday observance. All of my family get-togethers are planned to circumvent Shabbos and any Jewish holiday, major or minor. We tried one year to involve family members in building and decorating our sukkah, but building and eating in the sukkah with relatives who don't really see the need to observe Sukkos quickly became for them a nuisance and a waste of time. Why eat out in the cold when we've got a nice warm house and a dining room table?

Although avoiding family get-togethers on religious holidays might sound like taking the easy way out of a situation that can, with some effort, be successfully handled, for some families it's the only option. If you and your family are willing to make compromises so that you can spend this time together, it will work. But if you're not willing to make halachically permissible compromises (we'll discuss later on what these are), and if your family is uncomfortable, annoyed, or turned off by any display of religiosity on your part, it's best if you not come together on Shabbos or on Jewish holidays. It will just make everyone unhappy.

If you can get together with your family only a few times a year because you live far away from one another, it might be best to choose days that will allow you to spend enjoyable time together. You will still have to deal with the kashrus and modesty issues that are dealt with in other chapters. (The issues involved in getting together to celebrate life-cycle events such as weddings and bar mitzvahs are the subject of still another chapter.) Some families will simply find that Thanksgiving and Labor Day weekend are better options for getting together than Pesach and Rosh Hashanah.

Although the avoidance option is the safest one, what is lost is the opportunity to share happy times with your family in a Jewish context, to develop and continue family traditions, to share with your family what you have found to be so beautiful and meaningful in your observant lifestyle, and to show them how your children thrive in this environment. It saddens me that I can't share this with my family, but sometimes that's the way it has to be.

Families who have perfected the avoidance approach have essentially learned how not to fight. This is no simple thing, and in some families it is a major accomplishment, an act of love and commitment from all members of the family. To maintain a polite, respectful relationship in an environment that is potentially rife with conflict is also a positive thing, and far better than complete disconnection.

But on to more cheerful topics. The purpose of this chapter is to help you and your family confront and overcome—with love, understanding, flexibility, and respect—the difficult issues that arise when you spend Shabbos and Jewish holidays together. It's not as hard as you think.

OBSERVING SHABBOS AND HONORING YOUR PARENTS: CAN YOU DO BOTH?

As a newly observant Jew, you might be faced with two fundamental religious requirements that are equally important and equally beautiful but that sometimes can come into conflict with each other. It is no coincidence that in the listing of the Ten Commandments in the Torah, observing Shabbos, the fourth commandment, is followed immediately by honoring one's parents, the fifth commandment. The Torah realizes that there might be occasions when these two commandments come into conflict. What do you do in such situations? Let's begin by examining the laws of Shabbos, so that we can understand the philosophy behind them and their practical applications.

The Fourth Commandment: Observing Shabbos

None of the other 612 commandments is mentioned in the Torah as many times as the requirement to observe Shabbos. Unlike the prohibition against mixing meat and milk, for which no reason is given in the Torah, the commandment to observe Shabbos is accompanied in the text by God's reason for establishing a weekly day of rest.

The Torah portrays Shabbos as an anchor that infuses the entire week with holiness and beauty. "More than the Jews keep Shabbos, Shabbos keeps the Jews," goes the popular saying. I always smile when I see, plastered on the back of a car, the bumper sticker that reads HANG IN THERE, SHABBOS IS COMING, because I know that my husband lives for Shabbos every week. He so cherishes this time that he firmly believes he could not manage the stress of his weekday life without the infusion of rest and spiritual reconnection that Shabbos affords him.

The tensions that may arise between you and your family over Shabbos observance are not over the notion of a weekly day of rest, because most people can appreciate the beauty in that idea, but, rather, over exactly what the Torah means when it commands us to abstain from work on the seventh day of the week. For some families, watching television is restful, and what does watching TV have to do with work? Let's discuss how to explain these concepts of "work" and "rest" to your family, who may well think that you've taken this "day of rest" idea way too far.

Because the commandment regarding Shabbos observance is written in two slightly different ways in the listing of the Ten Commandments in Exodus and Deuteronomy, the commentaries on the Torah tell us that the laws of Shabbos observance fall into two categories, "remembering the Sabbath day" (as it appears in Exodus), and "guarding the Sabbath day" (as it appears in Deuteronomy). Remembering Shabbos is a "thou shalt" commandment. It includes such practices as lighting candles, making kiddush over the wine, and eating three Shabbos meals, and such customs as designating extra-nice clothing that you will wear only on Shabbos, indulging in the much-anticipated "Shabbos nap," and singing Shabbos songs at mealtimes. Since these practices are not restrictions, they will probably not be met with as much resistance from your family as the second category of Shabbos laws, the "thou shalt nots," which come under the category of "guarding the Sabbath." This is the aspect of Shabbos observance that your family may have difficulty with—all the things that Sabbath-observant people can't do on Shabbos, and that you won't be doing if you spend Shabbos with them.

What Exactly Is Work?

The most common understanding of Shabbos prohibitions is that "one may not work on Shabbos." I always wondered how this could be so, since clearly rabbis and cantors are working on Shabbos, and prohibitions against doing things like writing seem to have little to do with working. A more precise understanding is that because God created the world in six days and rested on Shabbos, we are commanded to keep Shabbos as a testament to God-the-Creator. Just as He created and then rested, so must we.

So how do we define "rest" in this context? I remember a rabbi at a religious retreat (Gateways) giving a very funny speech about how he was assigned to a room on the thirteenth floor in a hotel where he had to spend Shabbos. Since taking the elevator is prohibited on Shabbos, he was forced to walk thirteen flights of stairs every time he left his room or returned to it. At one point on his way up the stairs, he ran into a hotel worker who attempted to point him in the direction of the elevators. "I can't use the elevator today," replied the rabbi, noticeably out of breath from his long climb. "It's Shabbos, my day of rest!"

In actual fact, using terms like "work" and "rest" are not the most accurate ways to describe what is required of us on Shabbos (although we all appreciate a good Shabbos nap!). Observing Shabbos is really about the cessation of creativity. Just as God ceased creating the world on His original Shabbos, so must we cease engaging in creative acts. When we say that Jews must not work on the Sabbath, this is what we mean.

Now we need to understand what is meant by creativity. Does that mean no finger-painting or building a house on Shabbos? The Mishnah tells us about thirty-nine specific creative acts that went into building the Tabernacle—the sanctuary created by the Children of Israel in the desert after the exodus from Egypt, a precursor to the Temple built by King Solomon in Jerusalem. As we replicate God's cessation from creativity in our observance of Shabbos each week, we similarly must refrain from performing any of these thirty-nine creative acts.

In this context, creating means the steps involved in taking something that already exists and making something new from it. Look at some basic products and then at more complex ones, and then think about all the steps involved in getting from the one to the other. For example, what has to be done to change a sheep's outer covering into a suit? Shearing to get the wool, bleaching the wool to make it white, combing it, dying it, spinning it into thread, weaving the thread to make the fabric, and then sewing the fabric into a jacket and pants. Other examples include a seed that becomes a loaf of bread, or clay that becomes an earthenware pot.

But how does this list of thirty-nine prohibited actions—no weaving, plowing, tanning, shearing, or baking, for example—translate into not driving a car, turning on the lights, or watching a good movie? All other Sabbath prohibitions are derived in some way from the original thirty-nine. For example, one of these prohibitions is kindling a fire. Because it is the creation of a spark that actually starts your car and makes it go with the firing of spark plugs, makes your lightbulb glow, and brings the picture to the movie screen, all of these activities are forbidden.

What is important to communicate to your family is that all the things you can't do on Shabbos, which may well irritate and inconvenience them, are not an arbitrary list of don'ts that the rabbis made up. They originate in a clearly defined and enumerated system of laws that have their basis in the Bible (the Written Law) and are clarified in the Mishnah and Talmud (the Oral Law). Jews have observed the Sabbath for thousands of years by observing these same restrictions and their derivations. A modern invention such as a time clock that turns a lamp on and off may make it possible for Jews to keep the laws without as much inconvenience, but the laws themselves haven't changed.

The laws of Shabbos exist so that we can experience for ourselves, every week, a small-scale reenactment of the creation of the world and the joy derived from stepping momentarily back from the responsibilities of creation to marvel at what has been created. When you can explain, without defensiveness, that these Shabbos prohibitions come from an organized, clearly defined system of laws thousands of years old that are not your personal invention, your family may come to understand why you just can't "bend a little."

There are many accommodations you can make so that you can spend time with your family. Some we've already discussed in the chapter on kashrus, and we'll get to others in the chapters that are to come. But this "bending a little" falls within the parameters of what is halachically permissible, and it will never involve actually violating Jewish law. Helping your family understand that the dos and don'ts of Sabbath observance are actually a well-defined and detailed system of laws will help them understand why you, a shomer-Shabbos Jew (which actually means a Jew who guards the Sabbath), will not "bend," even a little, in any way that would violate the laws of the Sabbath. To you, even a little bending would be violating the word of God. Although you want to accommodate the wishes of your parents, you can't do so if it means doing that.

The Fifth Commandment: Honoring Your Father and Mother

One of the best ways to measure character is to observe how a person honors his parents and relates to the rest of his family. While maintaining a close relationship with parents, siblings, and children is regarded by most people as something to strive for, for the observant Jew family harmony is a religious requirement as well as a personal desire.

Most people are aware of the fact that one of the Ten Commandments actually requires us to honor our parents. It comes before "don't murder," which is number six, and "don't steal," which is number eight. In fact, many Bible commentators see this law as the link between the first four commandments, which deal with the relationship between man and God, and the final six, which deal with relationships between people. In honoring your parents you honor the people who created you, and thereby you honor the God who created us all.

So, what does it mean to respect or honor one's parents? Although the Talmud lists the ways in which we are supposed to honor and revere our parents, we understood that one mother may feel honored with a weekly phone call; another may expect, or need, to hear from you three times a week—or even every day. One father will be happy with a Hallmark card on his birthday, another with courtside tickets to see his favorite basketball team. In one home adult children will rise when their father walks into the room; in another family the father would be very uncomfortable with this expression of respect.

What is universal, however, is the hurt felt by parents when their children don't show up for family get-togethers. Your intention is not to insult your dad when you don't attend his seventieth birthday party, which is scheduled for Saturday afternoon, but it will be hard for him to understand this intellectually and to accept it emotionally. You want to honor your parents, and it hurts you when they have scheduled something for a time when it's practically impossible for you to participate because of your religious obligations. You feel torn, as if you are in a no-win situation.

The requirement to observe Shabbos even if it results in making your parents unhappy does not imply a callous disregard of your parents' feelings, should these two precepts ever come into conflict. Honoring one's parents is one link in a chain of laws and traditions that extends all the way back to the revelation on Mount Sinai. Whether or not your parents are observant has no bearing on the fact that you want to—indeed, must—honor them. Simply because they are a link in that chain that leads you back to Sinai, they merit your respect. According to the Talmud, parents are the visible partners in a person's creation. By honoring them, you are led to acknowledge the invisible partner in your creation—God Himself. I'd suggest that you find a way to share this idea with them. Often, your parents will assume that they are diminished in your eyes because of their lack of observance, that you feel that they are no longer worthy of your respect. It will come as a surprise to them that your respect and honor are not conditioned on whether or not they choose to be observant. Your respect and honor will always be there, because they gave you life.

HOW TO OBSERVE SHABBOS AND HOLIDAYS WHEN YOU ARE SPENDING TIME WITH RELATIVES WHO ARE NOT OBSERVANT

In addition to Rosh Hashanah and Yom Kippur, three festivals are mentioned in the Bible—Pesach, Shavuos, and Sukkos. The way you observe them is in many ways similar to the way you observe Shabbos. So we'll start by discussing Shabbos and these festivals, and then we'll touch briefly on Chanukah, a holiday (like Purim) of later origin that is observed differently than the Bible-based holidays and presents different issues.

THE "DO I HAVE TO?" QUESTIONS YOUR FAMILY WILL BE ASKING

Here's a scenario that might be familiar to you. Your parents have flown in from Arizona to take in some Broadway shows, visit some museums, and spend some time with all their children and grandchildren. Because of kashrus issues, everyone acknowledges that it will be easier if the whole gang spends the weekend at your home. But they're not very happy about it, because they don't observe Shabbos the way you do, if at all, and they're worried about what spending Shabbos under your roof will mean for them. What follows are a few questions your parents and siblings might ask you. Even if they don't ask you these questions directly, they will likely be thinking them (unless you long ago worked out with them the rules in your home). So you might want to be proactive and bring up some of these questions in advance.

1. I like to watch the ten o'clock news before I go to bed. Do I have to avoid doing so in your home just because you don't watch TV on the Sabbath? What if I'm in a guest room and you can't hear the TV if I have it on?

2. Do I have to light the Sabbath candles on Friday night? I don't do it in my own home, and I would be very uncomfortable doing it here.

3. It's wonderful to be together with everyone, but the Sabbath day is *so long,* and my visit here is so short. There are other things I want to do besides visit with my children and grandkids. On Saturday afternoon, can I get into the car and drive to the mall, or to a museum?

4. I don't want to go to synagogue, even if the whole family goes. Do I have to go, or can I just stay home and wait for all of you to come home for lunch?

5. What if I want to talk to Aunt Jean, who'll be calling me over the weekend to make arrangements for us to get together during the week? Can I answer your phone if I'm expecting a call?

6. My kids don't understand it when your kids tell them not to play with their Game Boy or their crayons on Shabbos. Do they have to observe these rules just because your kids observe them? The kids are too young to understand all of this. They just want to have fun! I don't want them to resent coming to visit you because they find it boring.

Holiday visits bring additional questions:

7. I like visiting your sukkah and seeing all the decorations that the kids made, but it's too cold outside for me to sit in it. Can I eat inside the house instead?

8. You know I don't fast on Yom Kippur—I never have, and I'm not going to start now. I'd be happy to watch the children to make the fast easier on you, or so you can go to synagogue. Do I have to sneak food so that they don't see me eating? Am I even allowed to eat in your home on Yom Kippur?

9. Do we *have* to hold off starting the Seder until after the stars come out? It's way too late. We sometimes don't get to the meal until ten o'clock, or later! And do we have to read the *whole* Haggadah? It's just too much. It makes the Seder something we dread instead of something we could enjoy together.

10. Do I have to make my entire home kosher for Passover just so you will come to us for the Seder?

11. It's always been my role as the father to lead the Seder. Do I have to turn this over to you, my son, because you consider yourself more knowledgeable about Judaism than I am?

BEFORE WE GET TO THE ANSWERS

Before answering each of these questions specifically, I'd like to review five basic principles of Shabbos and holiday observance. If your family understands where your answers are coming from, they may be able to answer other questions for themselves. And preparing yourself now, before these questions are asked, will help you feel more comfortable when they do come. Hopefully, the questions *will* come; always encourage your family to ask questions, rather than make assumptions.

Principle Number One: The Torah Requires Us to Respect Our Parents and Do Our Best to Satisfy Their Wishes

You can't violate religious laws to make your parents happy, but you can compromise on activities that have become part of your routine. If your parents will be bored by your usual talk about the weekly parshah at the Friday night table or by twenty minutes of singing z'meeros with your kids, you can skip or reduce these activities. What you'll be gaining in good will may be worth more than what you are losing. But I give this advice with one caveat: Don't skip these rituals because you assume your family will be uncomfortable. Who knows—they might love it! Or, at least, they might come to see what you love in it. Keep your normal practices at first, but if it's clear that some customs make your family uncomfortable, you can make some changes the next time around.

Principle Number Two: You Are Permitted—Indeed, Required—to Violate the Sabbath to Save a Human Life

Your parents might be surprised to learn that the commandment not to violate Shabbos is such a powerful one that if Rosh Hashanah falls on Shabbos, we don't blow the shofar. Why not? Because we are concerned that the shofar-blower might momentarily forget that it's also Shabbos, and carry the shofar into the street, which violates the law of not carrying on Shabbos. This is the case even though blowing the shofar is one of the most important parts of the Rosh Hashanah service! But as powerful a requirement as Sabbath observance is, the Torah teaches us that its laws are given to us to live by, and not to die in our efforts to fulfill them. In the case of a life-threatening medical emergency, you *must* use the phone, drive a car, rip open items in a first-aid kit, or do whatever else is necessary to save a human life. Alas, this exception doesn't apply to attending Grandpa's ninetieth birthday party on Saturday afternoon, even though you are told that it will just "kill him" if you don't show up. That's probably a bit of an exaggeration. It would be better to see if there's any way to convince your family to move the party to Sunday.

Principle Number Three:
You Cannot Benefit from
Another Person's Violation of Shabbos

What this means is that you can't eat food that was cooked on Shabbos, and if you're reading and the room starts to get dark, your sister can't turn on the light for you, even if she thinks that it's no big deal for her to do so. Some of these things you'll be able to work out with your family in advance, but others—such as your mom offering to change a lightbulb for you if it suddenly blows—you'll have to deal with, politely, when they come up.

Principle Number Four:
You Cannot Cause Another Jew to Violate
Shabbos or Any Other Commandment

You cannot help another Jew do something that he or she is not permitted to do on Shabbos. For example, unless it is for a medical emergency, you can't lend your car to your father to drive on Shabbos. But if you invite your parents for Friday night dinner and encourage them to sleep over, but they choose to drive home at the end of the meal, you haven't caused them to violate Shabbos because you gave them the opportunity to observe Shabbos, which they chose to decline.

This issue once came up for me when a family member staying with me over Shabbos asked me on Friday afternoon if I knew where the closest amusement park was, so he could take his kids there on Saturday. I didn't want to appear judgmental, but I had to say, "I'm sorry, but I'm not comfortable with giving you that information. What you do with your family on Shabbos is your business and not mine, but I'm not allowed to help you violate Shabbos."

Principle Number Five: If You Have Young Children at Home, You May Choose to Not Invite for Shabbos and Holidays Nonobservant Relatives Who Won't Accomodate Your Restrictions When They Are Visiting You

It's complicated enough to explain to your kids why you live your life one way and your parents, siblings, and cousins live their lives a different way. They will naturally ask questions like, "If Uncle Joe is Jewish, why doesn't he wear a kippah?" or, "Why does Aunt Miriam have a bag from McDonald's?" They might be really confused by the notion of their visiting cousins going to a water park in the middle of a hot Shabbos afternoon—and they may even be jealous. In the interest of not confusing them and not putting them into an awkward situation where their friends ask them questions that they might find hurtful or embarrassing, you can elect, for your children's sake, not to invite relatives whom you know will not compromise in their usual practices when they are in your home. The same goes for relatives who approach your children when you're not around and assure them that it's okay to cheat on the observance rules when you are not around.

This does not mean that "What will my religious neighbors think of me if my nonobservant parents drive away in a car on Shabbos afternoon?" is a valid reason not to invite your parents to your home for Shabbos, or to discourage them from coming if they ask to be invited. This type of distancing is permitted only to protect your children, not your ego.

THE ANSWERS TO THE "DO I HAVE TO?" QUESTIONS

1. *I like to watch the ten o'clock news before I go to bed. Do I have to avoid doing so in your home just because you don't watch TV on the Sabbath? What if I'm in a guest room and you can't hear the TV if I have it on?*

We don't check what goes on in every room in our home. We ourselves don't watch TV on Shabbos.

2. *Do I have to light the Sabbath candles on Friday night? I don't do it in my own home, and I would be very uncomfortable.*

All Jews are required to light Sabbath candles or make sure someone else discharges this responsibility for them. But if you are not comfortable doing so, I'll be happy to have you in mind when I light mine. If the only reason you don't want to light is that you don't know how to recite or read the blessing, you can light your candles when I do, listen to me say the blessing, and say "Amen." I'd love it if we could do this together.

3. *It's wonderful to be together with everyone, but the Sabbath day is so long, and my visit here is so short. There are other things I want to do besides visit with my children and grandkids. On Saturday afternoon, can I get into my car and drive to the mall, or to a museum?*

I'm not permitted to tell you that you can do something that violates Jewish law, even if you don't choose to follow those laws. You are, however, free to make your own decisions about what you want to do.

(If you have young children at home, you might reply: "I can appreciate that this is difficult for you, but I don't want to confuse my kids. I'm sure we can find a way to make the Shabbos day enjoyable for you. I'd prefer for you to stick around and not leave in the middle of the afternoon.")

4. *I don't want to go to synagogue on Shabbos, even if the whole family goes. Do I have to go, or can I just stay home and wait for all of you to come home for lunch?*

Sometimes a person doesn't feel up to going to shul. If you like, I'll stay with you; I can daven at home. (Staying at home with your parent is an option only if you're a woman. Men, as we will discuss in Chapter 3, should daven with a minyan.)

(Here's another possible reply: "We have a very warm and friendly congregation, and I know some of our friends would love to meet you. Why don't you wander over around eleven-thirty, when it's almost time for the Kiddush? Or would you like to attend our beginner's service? I learned so much there, and the rabbi who leads the service really makes it interesting. It's mostly in English and he explains a lot about the prayers. It's only an hour long and starts at ten. Would either of these options work for you?")

5. *What if I want to talk to Aunt Jean, who'll be calling me over the weekend to make arrangements for us to get together during the week. Can I answer your phone if I'm expecting a call?*

Please tell Aunt Jean that the policy in our home is not to answer a ringing phone on Shabbos, so we'd appreciate it if you and she worked out arrangements before or after Shabbos. If you need to use the phone for any sort of medical emergency (of course I hope you won't need to), you can certainly use any phone at all.

6. My kids don't understand it when your kids tell them not to play with their Game Boy or their crayons on Shabbos. Do they have to observe these rules just because your kids observe them? The kids are too young to understand all of this. They just want to have fun! I don't want them to resent coming to visit you because they find it boring.

It's important that we find a way for everyone to enjoy being together, and I'm sure we can do that. There are lots of permissible, fun activities that can be done on Shabbos, and I'm sure we can make them enjoyable for your kids. Every home has house rules, including yours. Our house rules for Shabbos and holidays are that there are certain toys that the kids don't play with. Why don't we put our heads together and figure out what Shabbos-appropriate games and activities we have that your kids would enjoy?"

(Most of the time, if a child asks, "Can I color?" and is told, "No, but here's something else that you can do," the child easily moves on to the other activity. But if, because they have issues with Sabbath observance in general, the child's parents view this as their kid being unreasonably deprived, that same "No, you can't color" can be the catalyst for a difficult and completely avoidable scene between the adults. These things should be worked out in advance. To begin with, it's a good idea to put away all nonpermissible toys before Shabbos begins. If this is the first time your family is getting together in your home for Shabbos, politely and tactfully review with them the ground rules and all the available alternatives before Shabbos begins. After that first time, everyone will have gotten the hang of it and it'll be easier the next time around.)

Holidays bring additional questions:

7. I like visiting your sukkah and seeing all the decorations that the kids made, but it's too cold outside for me to sit in it. Can I eat inside the house instead?

Yes, you can eat inside the house if sitting in the sukkah is going to make you uncomfortable. We're not required to eat in a sukkah if it will cause physical discomfort—if, for example, it's raining. If it's raining on the first two nights of the holiday, we just make Kiddush and eat a substantial piece of challah in the sukkah, and then finish the meal indoors. If we're lucky enough to have a beautiful fall day, I do hope you'll join us for a meal in the sukkah. It's a special time for us, and we'd really love to share it with you. I've got a warm coat for you and a blanket if that would help!

8. You know I don't fast on Yom Kippur—I never have, and I'm not going to start now. I'd be happy to watch the children to make the fast easier on you, or so you can go to synagogue. Do I have to sneak food so that they don't see me eating? Am I even allowed to eat in your home on Yom Kippur?

(Avoid the temptation to give Grandma a lecture about how fasting on Yom Kippur is one of the most important Jewish observances and that, yes, starting now comes under the category of "better late than never." As with all Jewish laws, your relatives are free to choose for themselves whether or not they will fast, and if so, for how long. The fact that they are in your home does not make you responsible for their observance or lack thereof. You might say something like this:)

You know how I feel about fasting on Yom Kippur, but this is something you have to decide for yourself. However, my kids have been taught that eating on Yom Kippur is a big no-no, and it would really upset them to see you doing so. If you do eat, it's important to me that you not eat in front of the kids.

AND ON THE TOPIC OF PESACH . . .

The next three questions deal with the Pesach Seder. Because Pesach observance includes many prayers, rituals, and kashrus requirements, there's a lot to be taken into consideration. Many books have been written solely on how properly to fulfill these requirements. If you are going to spend any part of Pesach with your family, you will definitely encounter more than the three questions listed here. The best thing to do is to consult your rabbi.

Many observant families have decided that because of the complexity and importance of the issues involved, the seder is not the place to negotiate compromises with nonobservant relatives. If what will result is a Seder that neither you nor your relatives will be happy with, it might be best for your relatives to have their own Seder in the style that pleases them, and for your immediate family to have your own Seder, even if it's just you, your spouse, and your kids—who will have plenty of Pesach material that they learned in school and will be eager to share with you. While having a Seder with your relatives can be made to work technically, in some situations it's just not the way to go.

If, however, you feel that you can explain your requirements to your family in such a way that you will all be able to enjoy the Seder, it certainly is a nice way for you to get together with them. Perhaps this will help.

9. *Do we have to hold off starting the Seder until after the stars come out? It's way too late. We sometimes don't get to the meal until ten o'clock, or later! And do we have to read the whole Haggadah? It's just too much. It makes the Seder something we dread instead of something we could enjoy together.*

Because the Jewish calendar was created with evening preceding morning, the new day doesn't begin until nightfall. If the Seder is begun before then, you are celebrating the Seder on the day before Passover. It's like celebrating New Year's Eve on December 30, or fasting on the day before Yom Kippur, because it's more convenient. I can sit down with you when you start the Seder at, say, six-thirty, but I can't myself begin until around nine. I can say "amen" to your Kiddush and join in the reading, singing, and conversation, but I can't make my Kiddush and begin eating the ritual foods until around nine. My younger kids can eat the meal with you, but I can't eat the meal until I get to that point in the Seder myself. You may read as much of the Haggadah as you are able. I'll be reading the whole thing, so I hope you'll bear with me.

10. Do I have to make my entire home kosher for Pesach just so you will come to us for the Seder?

I myself was surprised to learn that I can be in the presence of chometz on Pesach, so long as I'm not eating it and so long as I don't own it. I may enter a home that was not prepared for Pesach, but because you haven't cleaned and prepared your home for Pesach the way I've cleaned and prepared mine, I probably can't eat a lot of the kosher-for-Passover food you've brought into your home. Because your kosher-for-Passover food was cooked or heated up in an oven that was not properly kashered for Passover, and because it is being served on plates on which chometz has been served, I can't eat it. I appreciate all the trouble you went through to buy kosher-for-Passover food, but this is not an area in which I can compromise. I'll be bringing my own food, dishes, and cutlery. What would probably be easier would be if you'd all come to my home for the Seder.

11. It's always been my role as the father to lead the Seder. Do I have to turn over this job to you, my son, because you consider yourself more knowledgeable about Judaism than I am?

Even among families where everyone is observant, it's not uncommon to find adult or teenage children who are much more knowledgeable religiously than their parents. The true role of the leader is to pass on the family traditions from one generation to the next. While knowledge is important, it should not determine who leads the Seder.

Some fathers may take pride in watching their son lead the Seder, but even if your father would like you to do it, I'd suggest that your father still sit at the head of the table (unless your grandfather is present; then he would sit at the head of the table). It's a matter of respect. If you will be sharing responsibility for leading the Seder with your father, you might want to review the Haggadah together before the holiday begins so that at the Seder, everyone is figuratively and literally on the same page.

THE BOTTOM LINE ON PESACH

This is a very tricky area. Pesach has more rules associated with it than any other holiday, and its proper observance is something most observant Jews are particularly careful about. Yes, it's nice to have a Seder with your parents, siblings, and other extended family members, but it's possible that everyone will simply spend the evening being unhappy.

Another thing to keep in mind is your kids. Pesach is the most child-centered of all Jewish holidays. Indeed, it says in the Haggadah that one of the requirements is that "you shall tell your children" the story of Pesach. Children learn how to conduct the Seder by watching their parents do it. And they bring from school to the Seder adorable handmade Haggadahs that are full of information that they will be bursting to share with you. (Faced with our children's desire to share what they have learned with us, Stephen and I sometimes struggle to finish our seder by midnight!) If your Seder is full of tension—either because you want to hear every last bit of what your kids have to say and your relatives are thoroughly bored, or because you feel that your kids are being shortchanged because the Seder is being rushed to accommodate impatient relatives—your children's experience of the Seder will be negative rather than positive. This may have negative repercussions for years to come, when it is their turn to pass along the tradition to their own children.

If you are having the Seder in your parents' home, the best approach would be to fully discuss with your family way ahead of time what you can compromise on and what you can't, and see if they are willing to have the Seder with you under these circumstances. If you've worked out the concessions to everyone's satisfaction but you'd like to have one Seder where you don't have to compromise at all, look into the possibility of having the second Seder with an observant family in your parents' neighborhood.

If you are hosting the Seder in your home, your family can leave the Seder whenever they feel like doing so; this is certainly the easier option for you. And perhaps they won't find it so boring after all. They might well love all the clever insights your children bring to the table.

Now we shift gears to a different set of questions. While your family will ask the "Do I have to?" questions regarding things that they think you will make them do, you yourself will ask the "Am I allowed to?" questions regarding things that you thought were not permitted for an observant Jew to do on Shabbos and holidays. One thing to bear in mind is that this book is an introductory guide, and that you might want to discuss these issues in more detail with your rabbi.

THE "AM I ALLOWED TO?" QUESTIONS THAT YOU WILL HAVE—AND THE ANSWERS

1. Am I allowed to go to my parents for Shabbos if the television is always on and they flip the lights on and off all day long?

As long as you personally are not doing anything to violate Shabbos, you can stay there. If asking your parents to turn the TV off will make them angry, you shouldn't do so. Yes, having the TV on will disrupt your oneg Shabbos, your enjoyment of Shabbos, but you will not be breaking Jewish law. If you have a cordial and mutually respectful relationship with your parents, you can certainly request that the television not be on during Shabbos. They might well be accommodating and keep the set off if you have by this time succeeded in moving beyond making observance issues a power struggle. Your parents may want so much for you to visit that they will accommodate you in other ways as well, from bringing in take-out kosher food, to having the lights go off and on with time clocks, to making room in the weekend schedule for a Shabbos nap! If accommodations are made for you, never take this for granted. It's a great act of love for your family to disrupt their normal routine in order to make you feel comfortable.

It is important to note, however, that the overriding issue here is honoring your parents. This doesn't apply in the same way in the case of other nonobservant relatives, such as cousins. There's less of a justification to spend Shabbos with them, unless not doing so would make your parents upset, in which case it becomes an honoring-your-parents issue. If, for whatever reason, potentially upset parents are not involved, suggest that you get together another time.

2. *Whenever I visit my sister for Shabbos and I tell my kids that they can't do something her kids are doing, my sister says something like, "Why don't you lighten up while you're here? We don't believe in all of that stuff!" How can I stick to my commitments without turning every visit into a fight?*

First of all, if every Shabbos visit turns into a fight over observance, don't visit your sister with the kids on Shabbos! But let's say you live down the street from her and the cousins love getting together, so you want to make this work. It's important to determine where your sister's reaction is coming from. It might well be that you do need to lighten up—not in your observance, but in the way that you bring these issues to the attention of your children.

If you are screaming "Muktzah" at them, as if they have touched a poisonous snake, that could be off-putting to your sister, who doesn't understand what the big deal is about handling a box of crayons. Try a more positive approach, i.e., redirection, by saying something like "Remember, we don't color on Shabbos—let's play with this game instead." The good news is that unless your children are very young, they will soon enough know what they can't play with on Shabbos and will stay away from those things naturally.

It's quite probable that your sister simply does not know the halachic issues involved. In a society that stresses freedom of choice, it's not surprising that she might view your children as being unnecessarily restricted. That's why I wrote this book. You now have some good suggestions for how to explain to her why you do what you do (perhaps you can give her a copy of this book for starters!), so that the two of you can put an end to the conflict entirely. Although she may not join you in observance, she can come to respect why it is important to you and your children. Sooner or later, if your relationship is positive and your visits frequent enough, she may start putting away the muktzah toys before you arrive!

3. There is no synagogue within walking distance of the home I'm visiting on Shabbos. Am I allowed to go there if my only option is to daven alone in my host's home?

We are taught that a man should if at all possible daven with a minyan on Shabbos, particularly because the Torah is also read at that time. This is not an issue for women, as we will discuss in Chapter 3. If you are a man, consult your rabbi.

It is amazing to me to observe the lengths—literally—to which an observant man will go to attend shul on Shabbos. In one of our former communities there was a gentleman who walked more than five miles each way every Shabbos because there was no Orthodox synagogue closer to his home and he didn't want to move. He was there in rain, snow, or hot weather, a real inspiration to those of us who whined about walking a half-mile in the rain!

4. I'm spending a few days during the week with my parents, and my travel requirements are such that I won't be able to get back home in time for Shabbos, so I will have to spend it with them. They won't make any sort of accommodation for my Shabbos observance, but they do live near an observant community. What I'd like to do is sleep at their home but take my meals and spend most of Shabbos afternoon with a nearby Sabbath-observant family. Do you think this would work? Would my parents be insulted?

This depends entirely on your parents' personalities and on how they feel about your being observant. If you think they would be agreeable to it if you explained it properly to them, it's worth a try. Start off by saying how much you look forward to spending time with them during the week, and then remind them that your previous attempts to spend Shabbos together just didn't work out to anyone's satisfaction and would probably not work out any better now. If you don't spend a great deal of time with them on Shabbos, everyone will be left with the pleasant memories of the weekday visit, and none of the tension that would arise from your efforts to observe Shabbos the way you want to in a nonobservant environment. A nice thing to do would be to ask the family with whom you will be eating if they wouldn't mind calling your parents and inviting them for dinner on Friday night.

5. My kids are just starting to realize that their cousins do not share their observance practices, and that every Jewish kid in the world is not Sabbath-observant and kosher like they are. Is it okay for me to bring them into a nonobservant environment, where they might come to resent keeping Shabbos or keeping kosher because they see their cousins doing things that they are not permitted to do?

Every family will deal with this question differently, as

guided by their rabbi and by the way their own children deal with these situations. Let's face it, your young son pointing his finger at his cousin and saying to his face, "You're not Jewish. You aren't wearing a kippah!" is something we all want to avoid. Little kids often just say what's on their mind, because they aren't yet aware of all the consequences of doing so. The best way to handle this is to explain to your kids ahead of time what they can expect: that everyone they are visiting is Jewish (of course, this might not be the case if someone in your family has intermarried) but that these family members simply aren't observant like we are. At first your children will be fascinated, and maybe a bit upset, by the differences. Soon enough, though, kids being kids, they will work it out in their heads and just enjoy playing together with their cousins. If appropriate, you can also point out what your kids have in common with their cousins, such as celebrating Purim and Chanukah, or eating in a sukkah, rather than focusing on the differences.

As your children approach their teen years and the differences between them and their cousins come into sharper focus, they might feel uncomfortable around some of their nonobservant cousins. Don't force them into situations that would make them feel uncomfortable—when they get a bit older they may well feel differently.

6. Am I allowed to invite my relatives for Shabbos if I know that they will drive on Shabbos to come here?

There are rabbis who permit this, so long as your invitation specifies that you're inviting them to arrive before

Shabbos and sleep over on Friday night. However, this is a complex issue and there are different rabbinic opinions. You should consult your own rabbi.

7. My sister flies in four times a year for business, and she stays with us for Shabbos because she gets a better ticket price with a Saturday night stay-over. The problem is, she really doesn't enjoy or respect the way we observe Shabbos. She's unhappy the entire time she's here, and so are we. Part of me wants to tell her that she might be happier staying in a hotel, but I love her and I don't want to insult her. What can I do?

Of course, you don't want your sister to feel unwelcome in your home. But she's demonstrated to you that staying with you over Shabbos doesn't work for her, either. Maybe she would indeed rather be in a hotel but she doesn't want to hurt *your* feelings!

Discuss this sensitive topic with her in a calm and loving manner. Brainstorm for alternatives that would work for both of you. Maybe she could stay in a nearby motel or bed-and-breakfast and join you just for meals. (It would have to be possible for her to walk from the motel to your home; if she chooses not to, that's her decision.) Perhaps she can plan an activity for Saturday afternoon, so that she doesn't have to spend the entire day with you. You can say that, much as you'd like to spend the afternoon with her, if she wouldn't be happy doing so, you wouldn't be insulted if she chose to spend the afternoon elsewhere.

Talk this over with her before her next visit. Tell her you love her and enjoy spending time with her, ask her if she can be specific about what it is that bothers her when you're together for Shabbos, and see if there's a way to address it. Maybe she can handle most of it, but there's just one thing that really gets under her skin. She might be surprised at how flexible you can be, within certain limits.

8. My mother buys only kosher food when I come to visit for Shabbos, but then she cooks the food on Shabbos. Am I allowed to eat it?

No, you can't. Thank her tremendously for her efforts and then explain to her that Jewish law doesn't permit you to benefit from her violation of Shabbos, and her food is so delicious, you'd definitely be benefiting! Once you've explained this to her, offer to help her cook the food before Shabbos (and maybe even set up a blech or warming tray for her). If you've explained it properly, this question shouldn't come up again.

AND WHEN IT COMES TO THE HOLIDAYS . . .

9. My brother is getting the family together to celebrate his fortieth birthday. It falls during chol ha'moed Sukkos and he doesn't build a sukkah. What should I do about eating there?

Because eating in a sukkah is a time-based commandment, it's not something women are required to do, but men are. However, you are actually permitted to eat meat, fish, fruits, vegetables, and dairy products outside of the sukkah; more than a *kizayis* of grain-based food (i.e., wheat, oats, rye, spelt, and barley), on the other hand, must be eaten only in a sukkah. This is not the ideal situation; it's okay only if you have no alternative. Eat in your own sukkah before you leave for the party; if you get hungry while you're there, you can have a small snack from the permissible foods. If your family wonders why you aren't eating the apple pie, explain about the holiday requirements, assure them that you are not starving, and tell them it was important for you to be there for the birthday party.

If for some reason you must spend yom tov Sukkos with your family, see if you can find a synagogue-based sukkah nearby, or if you can be accommodated by a neighbor's sukkah. If that doesn't work, ask your family if you can bring a portable sukkah and set it up in their backyard. It's not expensive and it's not hard to put up. You can order one in a local Jewish bookstore or on the Internet. You'll be the talk of the town!

10. Am I allowed to attend my sister's Chanukah party if there's a Christmas tree in her home?

Some Jews have Christmas trees in their homes for purely secular reasons—because it's an American thing to do, or because all their neighbors have one. Some will have a small tree that they call a "Chanukah bush." If your sister's tree is not there for a religious reason, you can attend her Chanukah party.

If, however, the tree is there because her non-Jewish husband celebrates Christmas, or because the children are being raised as both Jews and Christians, this is a matter to discuss with your rabbi.

ON A PERSONAL NOTE

As a child growing up in my parents' home, I knew about Passover, Rosh Hashanah, Yom Kippur, and Chanukah. You could say I was a four-holiday-a-year Jew. What a shock it was for me to discover that Judaism has a holiday or two for almost every month of the year, and that Passover continues for eight days, not just one seder night!

Because I didn't attend Hebrew school, I had never heard of Purim, Shavuos, Sukkos, or Simchas Torah, for starters. In the early years of our marriage Stephen often took time off from work to observe the holidays fully, while I went back to work on the second day of Rosh Hashanah and ignored some of the "minor" holidays altogether. Over the years, as our children were educated in a Jewish day school and as we became a Sabbath-observant family, that all changed. We now observe every holiday, and I no longer categorize them in my head as "major" and "minor" holidays.

My children have been raised observant, or frum, from birth. (Actually, we coined our own expression for Sarah, our oldest. She's FFF, i.e., frum from five, instead of FFB, i.e., frum from birth.) My children have always known a rich Judaism that infuses every week with the beauty of Shabbos and every month with some celebration or another. They eagerly look forward to Shabbos, Rosh Hashanah, Sukkos, Chanukah, Purim, and all the other holidays. And for this gift from God, I am grateful every day. I wish this was something I could share with my family, but I've come to accept that they will make their own choices about how much of the Jewish calendar to observe and celebrate.

TO SUM IT UP

While Jewish law is very clear on what is and is not permissible on Shabbos and holidays, accommodations can be made. Hopefully, when your family gets comfortable with your commitment to observance and they see how far you are willing to extend yourself for their sake, they will meet you halfway. If, over time, you have established a good enough relationship with them, perhaps the day will come when they will accept and appreciate your Shabbos and holiday observance and will not ask you to modify anything when you're with them.

Keeping Shabbos and honoring parents originate from the same source: to help human beings shape their behavior with gratitude toward those who have had a hand in their creation. In the best of all worlds this flows both ways, with both God-the-Creator pleased with your observance and your other creators—your parents—proud of you as well.

Three

WHAT DO YOU MEAN, YOU CAN'T GO TO THE BEACH WITH US ANYMORE?

How to Explain the Laws of Modesty and Women's Issues

Somewhere down the road your family may be willing to concede that, when you view it from a certain perspective, there is a historic basis for the traditional observance of Shabbos and the holidays, and for keeping kosher. They may even acknowledge that a yeshivah education is not such a bad thing, and that there are some advantages to getting married at a young age. But it will probably take a great deal of explaining on your part to disabuse them of the popular belief among nonobservant Jews that Orthodox Judaism treats women like second-class citizens.

Whatever we believe, we all want to feel respected, loved, needed, fulfilled, and empowered in all aspects of our lives. And we all agree that all Jews—women as well as men—are entitled to central roles in both Jewish family and spiritual life. However, observant Jews believe that what the Torah and the Oral Law tell us about men and women—about the specific ways that God wants men and women to serve Him and carry out His plan for the world—creates a belief system and a way of life that, while it respects and empowers men and women equally, also acknowledges the fundamental differences between the sexes and the role these differences play in how we are supposed to serve God.

"EQUALITY"

It's right there in the Declaration of Independence: "All men are created equal." It's *the* founding principle of our nation, what set our country apart from the European monarchies from which our ancestors fled. And it took only about two hundred years for our government to acknowledge that women belonged in that sentence, too. Women fought hard for the right to vote, and continue to fight for an end to state-sanctioned discrimination in education and the workplace, and for equal pay for equal work.

When you tell your family that you have decided to become observant, one of the first things they may want to know is how on earth you can be part of something that makes women sit behind a screen in synagogue, doesn't allow women to be counted in a prayer quorum or participate equally in the synagogue service, won't permit a woman to be a rabbi or lead a prayer service, and makes women cover themselves up, obviously because men are depraved beings who can't control their thoughts or their actions.

As far as your family is concerned, these might well be medieval beliefs and practices that enlightened Jews abandoned a long time ago. They are willing to concede—because science tells them so—that there are physiological, behavioral, and psychological differences between men and women, but these differences should have nothing to do with how men and women serve God. They may view observant Judaism as a collection of repressive restrictions to quell primitive inhibitions, and a betrayal of the valiant struggle of generations of women who fought for women's empowerment; your own mother might well be one of those women who fought that battle. Your relatives may view the observant position on women's issues as the greatest example of the old-fashionedness of Orthodoxy and, therefore, the strongest justification for why Orthodoxy is no longer relevant for modern times. But, ironically, it is not uncommon to hear newly observant Jews explain that the Torah perspective on the roles of men and women was the most compelling reason for their choice of an observant path for themselves and their children.

You and your family agree on the basics: Everyone wants to feel significant, respected, loved, dignified, needed, creative, and empowered. All Jews agree that both men and women are entitled to respect, dignity, and a central role in Jewish family and spiritual life. You have more in common with your family than it might appear. What divides you is your belief about how women and men can best achieve those goals. Orthodox women believe with as much passion and fervor as feminists bring to the women's rights movement that the Torah-observant way of life is their best path to personal power. By dressing with understated elegance and being modestly covered, an observant woman feels valued and dignified. Most people are under the false impression that the laws of modesty are a collection of thou-shalt-not laws: Thou shalt not wear a miniskirt, thou shalt not dance in public, etc. But in fact, all these thou-shalt-not laws fall under one law: Thou shalt be dignified.

Almost all of the Torah's laws governing the role of women in Judaism are designed to preserve a woman's dignity and to avoid demeaning her. There are those who see in the laws of woman's modesty something similar to the way the Taliban treat their women. They couldn't be further from the truth. In contemporary society, when a woman refuses to allow herself to be seen or treated like a sex object, she may be considered a prude, but Torah Judaism wants a woman to see herself as full of dignity and worthy of respect—like the Torah itself, over which we place a beautiful covering when we are not reading from it. The Torah sees Jewish women as the inspiration for much of the spirituality in the world, and it sees modesty as the way women are infused with the power and holiness that the world depends upon.

That said, observant Judaism is of course concerned with more than just fulfilling personal goals; its primary focus is on how we can best serve God. Don't be surprised if your family has a hard time connecting the laws of modesty to serving God. It might even appear at first glance as if the Torah perspective is preventing women from serving God! Let's discuss how to explain this to your family so that they will at least understand you better, and perhaps even see some of the wisdom in these ancient but still entirely relevant laws.

THE TORAH PERSPECTIVE ON MEN AND WOMEN

For the Torah, the concept of "equality" between men and women is a nonissue because the Torah doesn't look at the relationship between men and women as one between "superior" and "inferior" beings. Judaism doesn't consider men "better" than women, or women "better" than men. The Bible is full of women, depicted in admiring terms, who played leadership roles and/or acted in what we would nowadays call rather proactive ways. But the Torah and the Oral Law also discuss at some length how men and women differ and how, as a result, what God requires of them differs.

The Oral Law tells us that women are born with an innate spirituality, a closeness to God, that men are not born with. It also says that women have intuitive understandings that men are not born with. Does this mean that women are "better" than men? That men are not capable of spirituality or intuition? No, it just explains how men and women are psychologically and spiritually different. It doesn't assign values; it simply uses this as a point of departure to explain the different responsibilities men and women have in serving God. The woman serves God by helping to imbue the rest of the world with her spirituality, and the man serves God by working to fill his life with more spiritual content and consciousness.

SO WHAT DOES ALL THIS HAVE TO DO WITH LONG SLEEVES AND WIGS?

After you have shared this philosophy and theology with your family, they might ask some pointed questions (and even if you never hear these questions because your family doesn't talk to you about these things, some family members will probably be thinking them, or discussing them with one another!). Any of these questions sound familiar?

1. Why can women watch men dance but men can't watch women dance, so that if there are men in a room, women in that room can't dance?

2. Why can men sing or chant from the Torah in front of women, but women can't sing or chant from Torah in front of men?

3. Why do women have to wear collarbone-covering, elbow-covering, knee-covering clothes, but men seem to be able to wear what they want, as long as they wear a kippah?

4. Why do married women have to cover their hair completely?

5. Why do women have to sit apart from men, and behind a mechitzah, in the synagogue?

6. Why are women "exempt" from fulfilling time-bound commandments in the Torah, such as putting on tefillin? What if they want to do them anyway?

7. Why can't women be included in a minyan (prayer quorum of ten)? You just said that men and women are equal in the eyes of the Torah!

8. Why can't women serve as the prayer leader or the Torah reader in communal prayer services?

9. Why can't women be ordained as rabbis? My female rabbi is as learned and effective as any male rabbi I ever met!

10. Why do women have to "purify" themselves once a month, after their menstrual period renders them "unclean"? Are you telling me that God thinks menstruating women are "dirty"? Is that how your husband thinks of you?

HOW YOU MIGHT RESPOND TO YOUR FAMILY WHEN ASKED ANY OF THESE QUESTIONS

1. Why can women watch men dance but men can't watch women dance, so that if there are men in a room, women in that room can't dance?

It's not quite that simple. When a man watches a woman dance, because of the way *most* women move when they dance, he is viewing her as a sexual object. When a woman watches a man dance, she is generally not viewing him as a sexual object. Would an observant woman be allowed to watch the men who dance at a place like Chippendales? No. The Torah prohibits women from performing in front of men because it diminishes their dignity. Torah Judaism teaches girls and women to see themselves in a regal manner; the role of women is not to serve as entertainment for men. That's why, at Orthodox simchas, women and men can dance as long as there is a mechitzah separating them. There's no prohibition against women dancing; in fact, observant women generally *love* to dance at simchas! They just don't want to be watched by men while they are doing so.

2. *Why can men sing or chant from the Torah in front of women, but women can't sing or chant from the Torah in front of men?*

The Talmud tells us that a woman's singing voice has an erotic effect on a man. Yes, men are expected to exhibit self-control over their feelings. Jewish law does not require women to appear in public covered in a sheet from head to toe. But the Torah also wants a man to avoid being in situations where he may have sexual feelings for a woman who is not his wife. Would you ever have found an observant woman at an Elvis Presley concert where he sings about being a "hunk of burning love"? No, and for the same reason.

I recently bought tickets for my husband to see a world-class drumming concert by a group of astonishing athletes who spend more than two hours performing athletic feats onstage. He has loved watching this group all of his life, but they usually perform on Shabbos so he can't see them. I was thrilled when I read that they would be playing locally on a Wednesday night, and I rushed to buy him a ticket. (They sell out almost immediately.) I myself have never seen them and I wondered, given the hefty price of one ticket, if I should buy myself a ticket as well. I asked the ticket seller, "Have you seen this group? Is it the kind of thing a woman can enjoy? Or is really a 'guy' thing, and should I just buy my husband a ticket and send him on his own?" His reply gave me my answer. "Well," he said, "if you'd enjoy watching a group of half-naked men wearing nothing but loincloths banging drums for a couple of hours, you should buy yourself a ticket. They are amazing!" I sent my husband alone.

The rule that forbids a man from hearing a woman sing or chant from the Torah in public may seem like overkill to your family. "Come on," they may say, "there's nothing sexy about a woman chanting from the Torah; that's ridiculous." The problem with a woman reading from the Torah or leading the prayers is that this is not regarded as modest behavior.

3. *Why do women have to wear collarbone-covering, elbow-covering, knee-covering clothes, but men seem to be able to wear what they want, as long as they wear a kippah?*

Whether you are religious or not, there are parts of your body that you cannot and will not display in public because society considers such display "indecent," i.e., erotic. The codes of Jewish law tell us that a woman's upper arms and thighs are erotic body parts, as is the torso below the neckline. Hundreds of years ago, this was regarded as a universal truth. But times change, don't they? For the world at large, perhaps. Observant Jews, whose guide is the Torah and not whatever happens to be currently in fashion, do not feel that they have to slavishly follow whatever secular society tells us is in style. In fact, to a young girl raised from birth to dress modestly, there isn't any other way. She would be horrified to go out in public "half-dressed," and she can't figure out why other women do so. "But there's nothing sexy about someone's arms; lighten up!" your family may say. "Precisely," you would respond, "that's the problem." Remember when *I Dream of Jeannie* first came on television in the 1960s, and there was a huge debate over whether or not it was okay to show Barbara Eden's belly button? Our society has steadily grown callous to the sensuality of women. Billboards, movies, and magazines reveal ever more parts of women's bodies; even nudity in a movie elicits barely more than a yawn. Now that we've gotten so used to seeing women half dressed, we have lost, as a culture, the ability to be aroused by something as simple as a woman's arm or a woman's hair. Orthodox Jews work hard to keep themselves from being influenced by the secular culture's modern attitude toward a woman's sensuality.

A note about women and pants: They certainly cover your thighs and knees, so what's wrong with wearing them? You may have female relatives who keep kosher and observe Shabbos and who wear pants. They might tell you that their rabbi says that loose-fitting pants can be considered modest clothing. Rather than debating who is right and wrong, appreciate the fact that you have relatives who keep kosher and observe Shabbos! Don't make an issue of their dress or their personal choice to wear pants. But if they want to know why you and your daughters choose not to wear pants, here are a couple of ways to explain it to them.

There are two issues involved: (1) The Torah tells us that a man may not wear women's clothing and a woman may not wear men's clothing. From their inception, pants were considered by society to be male garments. In fact, when women started wearing them at the turn of the last century, it created quite a scandal. Society eventually came to accept pants as a woman's garment, and your family doesn't think of pants as only a male garment, but that's not how strictly observant Jews view it. (2) Unless they are very loose-fitting, pants display the outline of a woman's figure. As we discussed above, an observant woman will not dress in public in a sensual way that might attract the attention of a man other than her husband.

Even if your family may eventually come to accept, and perhaps appreciate, the beauty and dignity of a knee-covering skirt and a modest neckline, covering a woman's hair is a whole different ball game. There are many Orthodox women who cover their hair only when praying in a synagogue, and with a hat or doily that doesn't cover all of their hair. This will confuse your family even more. They might say something like, "I have a neighbor who's Orthodox and she doesn't cover her hair all the time. Why do you have to?" So on to our next question.

4. Why do married women have to cover their hair completely?

The short answer is, See the answer to Question 3. The Talmud and, indeed, society at large tell us that a woman's hair is an erotic element of her body. There was a time when, in society at large, all women, married and unmarried, covered their hair in some way for that reason. Then only married women covered their hair, even if it was just with a lace cap. Then even married women stopped covering their hair. In recognition of the fact that a woman's hair may not be perceived as quite the same erotic element as it was hundreds of years ago, nowadays unmarried women are not required to cover their hair. But a woman's hair is still regarded as an element of sexual attractiveness (just look at magazine ads for shampoo and hair conditioner), and because a married woman is not supposed to be regarded in a sexual way by men other than her husband, married observant women cover their hair. That should absolutely *not* be understood to mean that they are supposed to look unattractive to everyone else. Observant women cover their hair with attractive hats, scarves, snoods, and even quite elegant human-hair wigs. Married women are encouraged to be attractive, but not attracting.

To expand this conversation beyond the sexual arena, your family might also find interesting another benefit that observant women get from covering their hair, one that is also quite meaningful to them. When an observant woman begins covering her hair after she is married, the act of doing so gives her a heightened feeling of spirituality. She feels imbued with a higher standard of religious observance, to compliment the fact that her hair is covered. Several years ago, when I began covering my hair, I was observing many more Jewish laws than ever before, but not all of them. When my hair was covered and I was tempted to do something that would not be appropriate for a Torah-observant woman, I would feel the contradiction and choose not to do whatever it was I'd been tempted to do. Instead of feeling restricting, covering my hair helped to solidify my identity as an observant Jew. Similarly, when a man wears a kippah in public, he's more careful about his behavior and speech because he recognizes that what he does will reflect on all Jews. Men who wear a kippah feel that it helps to remind them of their devotion to God and their commitment to observance. Many observant women feel the same way about covering their hair. This is something above and beyond sexuality.

5. *Why do women have to sit apart from men, and behind a mechitzah, in the synagogue?*

This question is one of the most heated ones you'll ever get from your family. The mechitzah can be, literally, the great divider. It's more than the physical separation between men and women during prayers; it also stands as a symbol of the philosophical divide between Jews of different levels of observance. I know this well, because I used to sit on the other side of the divide, and one of the greatest obstacles to my becoming observant was the negative association I had with the mechitzah. After years of davening in an Orthodox synagogue, I now appreciate everything I once disdained, but I understand completely how your family probably feels because I once felt the same way. Jews who have only a cursory understanding of the mechitzah may say something like this: "The mechitzah exists to keep men in line. But why should women be punished and be unable to see what's going on during the service just because men can't keep their thoughts clean while they are praying?" As is the case with a lot of the assumptions we discuss in this book, this is not really an accurate analysis of the purpose or structure of the mechitzah. A mechitzah can be designed in various ways and made of combinations of various materials so that a woman's view of the service is not obstructed. A mechitzah is not something that is intended to punish or demean women, but is more in the nature of a gift, whose purpose is to enhance the quality of prayer of both men and women. Here are some ways of explaining it that you might find helpful when your relatives ask you about it.

First, a simple explanation: A man should not pray or make a blessing over food in the presence of a woman who is immodestly clothed. Anyone is free to come into a synagogue during prayer services, regardless of how they are dressed. The existence of the mechitzah means that no one has to check every woman who comes through the door to make sure she is modestly dressed. So when your female relatives come to your shul for a family simchah or for Shabbos, they should dress modestly, but they don't have to wear high-necked, long-sleeved blouses, or long skirts. (They might feel more comfortable and less out of place if they dress modestly, and they may eventually realize this on their own. Or, if you have a good enough relationship with them, you can figure out a tactful way to mention this.)

The sources for men and women praying separately, either on opposite sides of a partition or with the women in a balcony, are found in both the Torah and the Mishnah. Everyone agrees that when you are praying to God, that should be the absolute focus of what you are doing. When you are sitting next to someone of the opposite sex in synagogue—whether it's the person you have been married to for thirty years or an attractive person you would perhaps like to date—you can get distracted from what you are really there to do. This isn't about men or women being unable to "control" themselves. It's about understanding how human nature works. Is it possible for a man to sit next to a woman and think only about praying to God? It's possible. But it's also possible that he will be distracted. And the same is true for women. Jewish law doesn't automatically assume the worst about people. It simply—and realistically—always takes all possibilities into consideration when formulating the law. Maintaining absolute concentration during prayer is difficult enough. What's the point of making it more difficult? When you're studying for an important exam, do you bring your books and notes to a sports stadium during a game? Or do you close the door to your room and put a big DO NOT DISTURB sign on it? "Don't put a stumbling block in front of a blind person," the Torah tells us. This sentence is interpreted to mean that it is forbidden to intentionally place someone in a situation where he or she might be tempted to violate Jewish law. The mechitzah exists to help remove stumbling blocks to prayer—and praying is, after all, what both men and women have come to the synagogue to do.

There is no law that says women must be stuck away in

the back of the synagogue, unable to hear the service or see the Torah being removed from the ark and carried to the table where it is read. Many synagogues make a special effort to include architectural elements that ensure that women feel that they are participating in the service. Synagogues where this is not the case most likely do not have large numbers of women davening there on a regular basis, and the women who do attend these synagogues are comfortable with the way their seating is arranged.

Even if your relatives may never feel comfortable davening in a shul with a mechitzah, perhaps if you explain it the right way they can come to understand why you now welcome it.

6. Why are women "exempt" from fulfilling time-bound commandments in the Torah, such as putting on tefillin? What if they want to do them anyway?

In traditional Jewish law and custom, the woman is the primary caregiver in the family. Therefore, according to the Mishnah, she is exempt from any religious requirement that would get in the way of taking care of her children properly. (A woman who is, for whatever reason, not a caregiver is also exempt from time-bound commandments.) Jewish law is not set up so that people face conflicting obligations and have to choose which one to fulfill. Men are required to pray at specific times of the day. Women are not similarly required to do so because Jewish law acknowledges that a woman may be occupied with taking care of her children when it is time to pray. This does not imply that praying is more important than taking care of children, or that taking care of children is more important than praying. It simply acknowledges that men and women fulfill their religious obligations in different ways. In fact, according to halachah, women should make every effort to pray at the proper times, particularly women who for whatever reason do not have family responsibilities. So what happens nowadays, when men and women share breadwinning and caregiving responsibilities? There's nothing wrong with this, but it doesn't change the Mishnah's view that, in the ideal world, the woman is the primary caregiver.

There is another, slightly more esoteric reason for a woman's exemption from time-bound religious obligations. Praying and performing religious rituals, such as putting on a tallis and tefillin, are designed to create a greater spiritual connection between God and man. As we discussed earlier, traditional Jewish theology says that women possess an inherent spiritual connection to God that men do not have. Therefore, women are not required to perform rituals designed to create this greater spiritual connection to God—but in some instances they may do so if they wish. Saying the blessing for the lulav and esrog on Sukkos and hearing the shofar on Rosh Hashanah are examples of time-bound obligations that women were not initially required to do, but that they have, over time, taken upon themselves anyway.

You can mention to your family that the Torah is not saying "Women *can't* do this," but, rather, "Women don't *have* to do this." But non-Orthodox Jews will probably still think this sounds like discrimination, and it won't be easy for you to help them see this any differently, even by explaining that modern, secular notions of "equality" have nothing to do with the way the Torah tells us that God wants men and women to serve Him. The Torah's idea of respecting women is not putting them in the untenable situation of having to choose between caring for their children and praying to God.

7. Why can't women be included in a minyan (prayer quorum of ten)?
8. Why can't women serve as the prayer leader or the Torah reader in communal prayer services?

Here's an opportunity to explain to your relatives that observant Jews do not view the prohibition on women being cantors or being included in a minyan as anything that has to do with issues of "equality." The reason is actually a very simple one, but not one that most people are aware of. Praying in a minyan is a time-bound commandment. Leading the prayers and reading from the Torah are components of this commandment. As we just discussed in Question 6, women are exempt from time-bound commandments. If you are exempt from a commandment, you cannot be used to fulfill it. For example, boys below bar mitzvah age are also exempt from praying in a minyan. If there are nine men and one ten-year-old boy in an Orthodox synagogue, they are still going to have to find another man to form a minyan.

Also, as we discussed in Question 2, women cannot lead a prayer service because it is considered immodest behavior.

9. Why can't women be ordained as rabbis?

According to Jewish tradition, the way a woman serves God is by being the primary caregiver to her children. If that is what she is doing, it is believed that she cannot possibly complete all the learning required to be ordained as a rabbi, and she cannot maintain the level of study involved in increasing her erudition and expertise. There are women nowadays who undergo intensive, specialized study in Jewish law relating to women's issues so that they can serve as advocates for women in rabbinical courts and are able to answer halachic questions women have regarding issues of niddah (more about this in Question 10). You could say that they are functioning in a rabbinical capacity in these roles, as are women who teach advanced-level courses in seminaries and adult-education classes in synagogues, women who make it a practice of visiting members of the congregation when they are sick, and women who, if they are licensed practitioners, counsel families. Actual ordination, however, requires a level of commitment to study that is not possible if you are your children's primary caregiver.

But what about after the children are grown? Or what if a woman, for whatever reason, does not have children? Why not then? Because a big part of a rabbi's job is getting up in front of people and speaking—most notably, when he delivers the weekly sermon in synagogue. This is considered performing in public, and, as we know from Question 1, a woman should not perform in public, in front of men. It's not considered modest behavior.

10. Why do women have to "purify" themselves once a month, after their menstrual period renders them "unclean"?

The problem here is with the terms "pure" and "unclean." They are inaccurate but, unfortunately, common translations of the Hebrew words *tahor* and *tamay.* These are religious concepts that do not have single-word English-language equivalents. Jewish law places the highest possible value on human life and also takes extraordinary care to respect and honor the dead. As a form of acknowledgment of the gulf between the living and the dead and the sadness that is felt that the dead no longer have spiritual lives on earth, when a Jew comes in contact with a dead body, he becomes tamay, which meant in ancient times that he was unable to enter the Temple area until he was made tahor through prescribed rituals. Nowadays, in the absence of the Temple in Jerusalem, a washing ritual replaces the Temple ritual, which is why you see observant Jews wash their hands when they leave a funeral or a cemetery.

When a woman menstruates, the basis for a potential life is expelled from her body. It is considered a life lost, and so the woman becomes tamay. She becomes tahor by immersing in the mikvah, a small, specially constructed pool of gathered rainwater, after her menstrual period has halachically concluded. When a woman is menstruating and until she has immersed in the mikvah, which is called being in the state of niddah, she and her husband are required to avoid intimacy. Acknowledging that physical contact may lead to a desire for sexual intimacy, a husband and wife do not touch at all during this period, and may not even share the same bed.

Many books have been written about the unparalleled spiritual uplift and personal sanctity a woman who observes the laws of niddah and uses the mikvah feels. Because of the enforced separation of husband and wife during the niddah period, it also has the side benefit of enhancing both the sanctity and the passion of their marriage. When a woman is a niddah, she and her husband focus on nonsexual ways of communication—on the spiritual, intellectual, and companionate elements of their relationship—and on nonsexual ways of enhancing their lifelong partnership in every sense of that word. It's particularly unfortunate that a religious obligation that is so sensitive to the needs and desires of a married couple, that is designed to respect the holiness of observant Jews and to enhance the spiritual and physical elements of marriage, is denigrated by a complete misunderstanding of its rationale. If you have the opportunity to discuss what you find beautiful in these marital laws with relatives who ask you about them, it can be a satisfying experience. On the other hand, some relatives will just never want to go there. There's not much you can do about this, so in those instances you'll just have to keep the whole subject private.

ON TO MORE PRACTICAL ISSUES

Because contemporary society is so at variance with traditional Jewish theology regarding the differences between men and women, don't expect your family to feel all that differently after you have explained any or all of the above to them. There's nothing you can do about this, either. All you can do is present a positive example. If your relatives see that your marriage is a true partnership of equals, that you and your spouse support and respect each other, and that their sister, daughter, or daughter-in-law does not feel like a put-upon, second-class citizen, hopefully they will come to realize that this is because of the way you have chosen to live your religious lives as a couple and that you are happy with your decision. Remember, what your family wants most of all is for you to be happy.

On a more practical level, issues of modesty and modest behavior are going to come up when you spend time with your family, and you'll have to be prepared to deal with them. Let's discuss some common issues that might arise, ranging from what's playing on the television to how to handle the celebration of your aunt and uncle's fiftieth wedding anniversary at the country club that includes a fun swim for all.

It may come as a surprise to your relatives to learn that, for the observant Jew, issues of modesty are not confined to one's wardrobe. Until now we've been primarily discussing modesty as it relates to clothing and to men and women praying separately in the synagogue. These laws focus on how we may affect others with our dress and behavior. But issues of modesty also play a role in how much of the secular world observant adults are willing to expose themselves to and how much of this world they are willing to expose their children to. Observant Jews will intentionally place barriers between their children and elements of contemporary popular culture to keep their children from being exposed to certain lifestyles, images, and values that they feel will harm the Torah-observant life they are trying to build within their home.

It's hard enough to instill Torah values in children and maintain the sanctity of marriage in a completely religious environment, let alone one that is continually encountering pressure from the secular world to adopt ways of behavior that are antithetical to Torah values. Contemporary media—in all their forms—bombard us with these kinds of images and behaviors, and therefore many observant Jews severely limit the types of media that they allow into their homes. This might become an issue when you get together with your family.

A wide range of responses exists within the observant community regarding how to deal with unacceptable aspects of popular culture. Some families refrain from buying any type of secular magazine or newspaper; some simply avoid tabloid-type newspapers and magazines; some don't feel that the print media are as problematic as electronic media. Some families don't own a television; others do own one but strictly limit what their children may watch on it. All families with VCRs and computers stringently monitor what their children watch on them; some will prescreen secular movies, others will permit only videos with Jewish content. There are no hard-and-fast rules for every observant home, but within each home the rules tend to be pretty strict relative to the world around us. This is not to say that secular parents do not lay down similar rules for their children, but your relatives may discover that your rules are stricter than theirs.

SPENDING TIME TOGETHER AT YOUR HOME

This is the easiest option for family get-togethers. If you have a television, you might have to politely explain to your nephews and nieces that there are certain programs you don't watch, but there are plenty of others to pick from. The same goes for videos that your relatives might want to rent for family viewing. Generally, this needs to be discussed only once; for subsequent visits it will be understood. If your relatives are sensitive enough to ask if there is any particular way they should dress, you can tell them that you'd appreciate it if they didn't wear very short shorts and skirts, and halter tops. Some of your relatives will understand that you feel much more comfortable around them if they are more modestly dressed, and they will do so on their own. But other relatives will simply dress the way they want to dress. You will have to tactfully explain to them what is and is not appropriate dress in your home.

SPENDING TIME TOGETHER AT YOUR RELATIVES' HOME

The whole family has gathered at your parents' home for the annual Fourth of July barbecue. The kosher food, paper plates, plastic utensils, pots, and aluminum foil have been prepared well in advance, and your parents know how everything is to be served. So everyone can sit back, relax, and have a good time, right? Not yet; some additional advance planning is required. Your dad has just bought a new plasma TV and is eager to show it off. How can you make sure that your kids will not be settling down to watch something that you would find inappropriate? Simple—politely and tactfully mention to your parents a few days before you are scheduled to arrive that you prefer not to have your children watch certain kinds of television programs, and discuss with them what would make you feel most comfortable. Don't make them feel that there's anything "wrong" with what they like to watch. It's their prerogative to watch what they choose. If your parents plan to rent a movie for a family screening, again, very politely ask if you can have some input regarding what is chosen. These kinds of conversations have to happen only once or twice, and then your family will understand what your parameters are.

If this kind of advance discussion won't work for your family, or if you simply don't want your children to watch any television or any sort of movie, you will have to explain to them before you leave home that even though their cousins will be doing this, it's just not something that our family does. Make sure to bring along enough games for them to occupy themselves with.

You could certainly try explaining to your family that you sincerely value the time you are all getting to spend together, and do they really want the children to be glued in front of the television set instead of playing together? If you emphasize your desire to develop and maintain real family connections rather than making this about who's right or wrong about television-watching, you might find your relatives agreeing with you.

There are two ways you should *not* approach a family disagreement about television- or video-watching. The first is by marching over to the TV, turning it off, and lecturing whoever is watching about the horrors of contemporary television, how it will rot their children's brains or turn them into Jell-O. You may in fact believe this is so and your family may know that this is how you feel, but lecturing your relatives will accomplish nothing. (If they ever express their approval of how your kids are turning out, you can mention that you attribute it, in part, to your policy on television watching.) The second way not to approach a problematic television or video situation is by going along with whatever everyone else is doing so as not to create waves. If you don't allow your kids to watch PG-13 or R-rated movies at home, they should not be watching them at your parents' home, either.

There's nothing you can do about how your siblings and/or nieces and nephews will be dressed. If someone is wearing something particularly revealing, think very hard before you decide to say something about it. If saying something will cause a family crisis—which it might well do—it will just be counterproductive. You'll probably communicate your discomfort much more diplomatically by not saying anything but looking terribly uncomfortable, or by quietly sending your kids into another room to play.

The most important thing is *not* to make a scene, because it will have the exact opposite effect from what you have intended. If you see your nephew sharing his *Sports Illustrated* swimsuit issue with your son, steer your son away by simply saying that in our home, we don't look at such magazines. You might mention later on to your nephew's mom or dad that you would prefer it if your son was not exposed to these kinds of magazines when you come to visit. It is, however, their home, not yours, and there is only so much you can control. Over time, as your family becomes more familiar with your preferences, they will, hopefully, accommodate them to the best of their abilities. You may have some relatives who just aren't interested in being accommodating, who think the rules you have set down for your children are unnecessarily restrictive. If you feel uncomfortable spending time in their home, you can offer to host them in your home.

SPENDING TIME WITH YOUR RELATIVES AWAY FROM HOME

If your family wants to have a get-together at a beach or water park, you will have a tough decision to make. I know many families that really struggle with this issue as their children grow older and their families choose such venues for get-togethers. They feel torn between not wanting to alienate and upset their families and the need to protect their children from being exposed to, literally, too much exposure!

One option is to offer to meet your family afterward for dinner. Another is to suggest an alternative to the beach or water park, and explain that you're doing so because you really want to spend time with them. Some observant Jewish women will stay at a beach or participate in water park rides while fully clothed. Either they won't let their kids swim or, if they do, they'll make sure their younger daughters are wearing oversized T-shirts. (This would not be appropriate for older girls, and Jewish men and boys would avoid the situation completely by not attending.) All of these compromises are awkward at best. As your kids get older, they will be uncomfortable being in such an immodest environment. If you explain this the right way to your family, they may be willing to accommodate you by finding an alternate venue for the family get-together. Suggest alternate venues that would be appropriate for you can be just as much fun.

Even something as innocuous as a shopping trip can cause problems if you don't properly prepare for it. If your mom wants to treat you and your kids to a back-to-school shopping spree, try to stick with stores in your neighborhood that you are accustomed to shopping at, stores where you know that all the clothes will be appropriate. If, however, you'll be going to the mall near your parents' home, you will have to be prepared for the possibility that Mom will pick up an adorable sleeveless blouse or short skirt, hold it up against your daughter, and say, "But she'll look so cute in that! Come on, she's just a kid!" Nothing will be accomplished by losing your temper, except that you will create strife and tension within your family. Smile and say something like, "Yes, Mom, it's certainly a cute outfit, but we don't choose to dress this way, none of her friends dresses this way, and I know you can respect that. I'm sure we can find something just as cute that she can wear. Let's keep looking, okay?" Once your kids are old enough to communicate this, they'll let Grandma know on their own that they feel most comfortable dressing modestly. Because what Grandma wants more than anything is to make her grandchildren happy, she'll figure out pretty quickly what will accomplish that.

TO SUM IT UP

More than food, holiday observance, education, or courtship rituals, the traditional Jewish laws about what constitutes modest behavior and modest appearance, and the way Jewish law views the differences between men and women, might cause much heated conversation between you and your family. Or it may result in no conversation at all because it's a topic that your relatives avoid discussing with you but spend a great deal of time discussing among themselves.

Look at modesty laws from your family's point of view: When you remove the Torah and halachah from the equation, it makes perfect sense for them to be concerned that you are adopting a way of life that they feel is outdated and that seems to demean women. The most important message you can convey—and this will take more than just one conversation with them—is that, as an observant woman, you do not feel denigrated by your status in Jewish life; you feel uplifted. You feel honored, needed, treasured, and holy when you follow what Jewish law tells us about a woman's role; modest dress and behavior make you feel good about yourself. Hopefully, over time, your family will observe the joy and fulfillment your way of life gives you, the feeling that radiates out from within you and makes you feel truly beautiful.

Your goal should be achieving harmony within your family. Most of the tension surrounding modesty issues and women's issues can be eased by taking a respectful, friendly, and even humorous—when appropriate—attitude toward the whole subject. In other words, lighten up about it. When kept in perspective, modesty concerns do not have to be a barrier to your spending enjoyable time with your family. You just might have to miss the occasional family beach vacation.

ON A PERSONAL NOTE

As I evolved from nonobservant Jew to Orthodox Jew over the past twenty years, I can mark the transition most clearly by my changing feelings about the mechitzah in the synagogue and by my growing understanding of the ways traditional Judaism respects and empowers women.

As a nonobservant Jew, I never went to synagogue. (Well, my parents did force me to attend a few High Holiday services.) As a teenager and young adult, my focus was on how to make myself attractive and find a boyfriend (the shorter the skirt, the better), and how to excel in my studies so that I would have a successful career. During the 1970s and 1980s the feminist movement was gaining momentum, and I believed that I could be anything I wanted to be. I knew I wanted to get married, have children, and have a career. Where did Judaism fit in? I had no idea, and little interest in finding out.

I did eventually want to identify Jewishly in some way, however, so I became an active Reform Jew in my early thirties and joined a Reform temple in Massachusetts. The freestanding seats were arranged in a circle instead of pew-style, and during the last twenty minutes of the service everyone stood around the bima with their arms around one another, singing. Women played prominent roles in the synagogue's leadership, including a female cantor with a beautiful voice. The adult bat mitzvah program was popular, and it was when I completed the study program and created a bat mitzvah celebration for myself that I changed my name to Azriela. The women wore kippot and tallitot, and I bought myself a beautiful lavender set from Israel. I remember feeling very empowered as a woman there. But later on I began to feel that, on a spiritual and religious level, there was something missing in all of this.

Then I married Stephen. He was raised in a traditional Conservative home, and he was uncomfortable with many aspects of the Reform service. So when we relocated to a new community, either he and I would attend Conservative synagogues together, or he would daven alone at the Orthodox synagogue. I wouldn't set foot into that synagogue: I was very attached to sitting with my husband during the service, and the exclusive use of Hebrew in the Orthodox service just didn't work for me.

When we were in our early forties, Stephen and I decided to become a Sabbath-observant Orthodox family and to attend only an Orthodox synagogue. For him, the transition was an easy one. It was what he had been wanting all along. For me, however, this was a daunting challenge. I had to face all my fears and negative preconceived notions about Orthodox beliefs and practices. But I stuck with it because I had become convinced that being a traditional Torah-observant Jew was the right path for me, and that raising our children as observant Jews was the right thing to do.

What happened over the next two years shocked me. I came to prefer davening behind the mechitzah, apart from the men. I was no longer distracted by worrying about what my husband was thinking and feeling. I liked being surrounded by women when praying. I began to feel more attractive in my long skirts and modest outfits than I'd ever felt in my miniskirts. And although I expected to feel like a second-class citizen, because I thought I had just joined some male-chauvinist, antiwomen kind of club, I was in for a very pleasant surprise. As an observant Jewish woman, I came to feel truly honored and respected—by my husband, my children, and my community. No one could have been more surprised than I that this feeling was possible within Orthodox Judaism.

Orthodox Judaism did not bind me and my daughters with a long list of outdated restrictions that clipped our wings. On the contrary, it freed us to feel good about who we really were. It is not my purpose with this book to convince men or women to become observant Jews. But I do hope that this chapter will help Jews of all kinds to understand what it is that Orthodox women value about the way they live their lives, and why they feel that this lifestyle is empowering, sanctifying, and fulfilling. The mothers and sisters of observant women can stop worrying about us. We're in a good place.

Four

WHAT DO YOU MEAN, YOU'RE GETTING MARRIED? YOU'VE JUST MET EACH OTHER!

How to Explain Observant Dating Practices and the Observant View of Married Life

If you are newly observant and unmarried, your dating practices—even more than keeping kosher or dressing modestly or observing the Sabbath—will probably be one of the initial sources of conflict between you and your family. So why didn't I start the book off with this chapter? Because within the first three chapters are explanations of some of the fundamental beliefs of observant Jews and advice on how you, in turn, can explain these beliefs to your family and deal with the conflicts that these beliefs may create when you are together with your family. It would be very hard for your family to understand the observant perspective on dating and marriage without first understanding how central the Torah and Jewish law are in lives of observant Jews, and the effect they have on virtually all aspects of your life. I hope the first three chapters began to paint a clearer picture of this.

The conflicts that arise because you keep kosher and your parents don't, or you observe Shabbos and your parents don't, or you dress differently than your parents pale in comparison to the emotional storm that can be set off in your relationship with your family when it comes to a decision as life-changing as getting married. If your parents dislike or disapprove of your spouse, your relationship with them could be damaged to the point of complete disintegration. Alternatively, your relationship with your spouse could be strained to the point where it starts to threaten the stability of your marriage.

PARENTAL APPROVAL

We all crave our parents' approval. Whether you are a ten-year-old running home to show Mom and Dad a report card with all A's on it or a young adult who's just landed your first job in a prestigious firm, you want to hear your parents say, "Well done. We're proud of you."

When you have found the person with whom you want to spend the rest of your life, you want your parents to love this person, too—to approve of your choice and welcome him or her into your family. This has nothing to do with how observant you are or how nonobservant your family is. You still want them to get to know your fiancé and hear them say, "He's wonderful. We understand why you're so crazy about him. We know he'll be a lovely addition to our family."

If your parents don't approve of the person you're going to marry, it hurts. You can't help but think: Does this mean there's something wrong with my parents or there's something wrong with my fiancé? A lot of painful feelings may be expressed—or may be left unsaid. Unless your parents eventually do come around and in some definitive way indicate their acceptance of your spouse once you've married, these feelings will never go away. This will affect how much time you decide to spend with your family after you are married and how you relate to one another when you are together. Family get-togethers will become times of tension and surface politeness. And, of course, this will also affect the kind of relationship your children will have with their grandparents—if, indeed, they have any relationship at all.

The dating and courtship practices of observant Jews are very different from those of nonobservant Jews. You will expend great effort to explain the laws of kashrus and Shabbos to your family so they understand why these laws are so important to you. In the same way, you will have to explain the laws and customs of dating and courtship to your family *before* you introduce them to the person you are going to marry, so that when they meet this person they will be able to relate to him or her simply as a *person* and not as a *symbol* of a way of life that they may think is weird, medieval, or harmful to your future well-being.

WHY THIS CAN BE SO PAINFUL FOR YOUR PARENTS

No matter how hard you've tried to explain to your parents that your new, observant lifestyle is not just a passing "phase," they may continue to cling to the possibility that someday you'll change your mind and go back to being just like them. But when you announce one day to your parents that "there's someone I'd like you to meet," and a few days later in walks a person who is obviously as observant as you are, your parents will be forced to realize that this is not a passing phase. This is how you are going to live the rest of your life, and this might well be the person with whom you are going to live it. In this scenario what they will be seeing is not the wonderful person you want them to love as much as you do, but an abrupt end to the hope that you are ever going back to the way you were. With this in mind, no wonder they aren't exactly on board right away!

After you've spent a few strained hours together, during which your beloved has exhibited all the beautiful qualities that make people fall in love with her as soon as they get to know her, what you want more than anything else is for your mom to give her a kiss on the cheek and say, "It's been so nice getting to know you. I hope we see you again soon." But doing that means she is also saying, "It's fine with us that our son has become observant, that he is going to marry someone as observant as he is, and that before long he will be presenting us with observant grandchildren." That's a lot to expect after a two-hour meeting. If it doesn't happen, it doesn't mean your parents don't like her, or won't ever like her. It just means they are still taking it all in. They need time. Let them have the time they need.

Hopefully this won't happen, but if your parents are still having a hard time getting used to the idea that you are now observant, you should be prepared for the possibility that this meeting will reignite the arguments you may have had with them when you first told them about your decision to become observant. If you think this is a possibility, don't just "spring" your fiancée-to-be on them. Spend some time discussing this with them first, before you arrange for them all to meet.

You want your parents to be able to evaluate your beloved as a human being, not as an indicator that they have lost the battle for your soul. Observant or not, your parents know you better than anyone else in the world. You are right to want to know what they think of the person you want to marry. Just make sure you have done everything possible to ensure that they are evaluating a person and not a religious worldview that they don't share with you.

Conversely, if your parents carefully point out to you some qualities in your potential life partner that they find unsettling or unattractive, you are doing them a great disservice if you assume that, because they themselves are not observant, they will automatically disapprove of any observant person to whom you introduce them, and so you should just ignore anything they say. Pay attention. There could very well be wisdom in their words. It is possible that the unique radar that parents have when it comes to their children will pick up a character trait in your fiancé that you haven't noticed or that you are ignoring but that your parents, after many years of marriage, understand could be troublesome. If you've been raised by loving parents who have weathered the challenges of an enduring marriage, they do have something to teach you about it, even if they don't understand your religious observance.

When you find yourself closing your mind to your parents' input, replace the thought *"My parents are so against my being religious, they will never give my intended partner a fair shot,*" with something more like "*My parents have loved me and raised me: Who is better equipped to help me find someone with the kind of personality and character that will make me happy?*"

If you aren't bringing home a fiancée but are starting to introduce your parents to someone you are dating, help your parents get involved. You might say something like, "This girl is really outgoing, but loud. Do you think a quieter girl would be better for me?" There are no religious implications in this question, and it doesn't push any buttons. Whenever you can talk with your parents without pushing the observance alarm buttons, it helps to bridge the gap between you. Newly observant young adults don't spend enough time seeking nonreligious-oriented advice from their parents, advice that could serve as a bridge to communication. Instead, they may dwell exclusively on the religious qualities of their fiancé, in the hope of achieving acceptance from their parents for their observant lifestyle.

You'll have to realize that the person you are dating probably has some wonderful qualities about which your parents will not be as enthusiastic as you are. Yes, it's admirable that, after an eight-hour day at the office, he attends a Talmud class several evenings a week. Your parents just won't be as thrilled about this as you are, so find some other wonderful quality to mention to them, like the volunteer accounting work he does for his synagogue. If you can separate out religious issues, your parents could become your greatest allies in your search for the perfect spouse—or at least enthusiastic supporters of whomever you choose. But their attitudes will be affected by how you choose to handle this tricky time in your relationship with them and by what you choose to communicate.

HOW DO WE KNOW IF HE'S RIGHT FOR YOU? WE DON'T EVEN KNOW WHO YOU ARE ANYMORE!

Your parents have met him a few times by now. They're a little taken aback by the beard, but you sense that they like him. You're sure this is it, but you want to know if they feel the same way. So you ask them, straight out, "Okay, what do you think? Is this the guy for me?" Your dad looks at your mom, then looks down at his shoes and doesn't say anything. Your mom stares at the picture of you from your high school prom that hangs above the sideboard. You're starting to get worried. Finally, your mom clears her throat. "Honey, he's a wonderful young man. But you were captain of your soccer team in high school. For four years you didn't date anyone who didn't play soccer. You used to star in your school musicals. Look at the picture of you dressed up for your prom. You wouldn't be caught dead in a dress like that now. We just don't know you anymore. We don't know what kind of person would be right for you. We want to help you, but we can't."

Look at this dilemma from your parents' point of view. In many ways, you do appear to be a completely different person. Many of the activities that were important to you before you became observant have vanished from your life. The friends from high school with whom you used to hang out at the beach think you have lost your mind. You have a whole new group of friends. You used to go to rock concerts. Now you go off on weekend religious retreats and come back bursting with an enthusiasm that your parents find bewildering. Even something as simple as going to the movies with your mom becomes an ordeal, as you have to check to see if there's anything playing that's religiously suitable and not intended for four-year-olds. Your parents don't think that there's anything wrong with the way they raised you. But you appear to have taken that entire upbringing and thrown it into the trash with your soccer uniform.

Your parents need to know that in many important ways you are the same person over whom they lavished so much love and attention when you were a child, and that they do still know you—more than they think they do. You still hate broccoli, and you still love potato chips so much that you can't stop eating them once you start. You still have a hard time getting out of bed every morning. You dream of raising a family in a nice house in the suburbs, just like your mom always wanted for you. And you worry about making a living and about keeping yourself fit and healthy the same way your dad does. You still care about politics, and you're not much in favor of another Wal-Mart coming into town. You still enjoy cooking and reading (even if your literary tastes have changed) and you still make beef Stroganoff (but with parve sour cream). You are easily hurt by an insulting remark, just as you were in elementary school, when your mom would be there to comfort you after another kid was mean to you.

Many of the endearing qualities and familiar idiosyncrasies that define you to your parents are still there. But to your parents, your new persona—"observant son" or "observant daughter"—now appears to be such a huge part of who you are that all your other, more familiar traits seem to have vanished.

Here's something else your parents need to know. You are grateful for everything they have given you: the moral and ethical values; the appreciation of friends and family; the dog you got after you fell off the monkey bars and broke your arm; the passion they instilled in you to be true to your beliefs and ideals, which was what got you interested in exploring an observant lifestyle in the first place. It's your responsibility to make your parents understand that the person you have become has naturally developed from the child that they raised and is in fact an expression of, and not a departure from, their influence. Your parents do not expect you to be frozen at the point you were at when you first left the home. They recognize that once you have grown up you will have had new experiences and acquired new knowledge, and as a result you will chart you own way in life. What your parents hope to see is that the path you've chosen to take in life is at least a trail that can be traced back to the initial road that was paved by them. Is it possible that it was the upbringing by a dedicated, hard-working father that taught you to persevere in unraveling Talmudic complexities? If so, tell him so!

The importance you attach to living an observant life can be misunderstood by your parents to mean that you think that your life before you became observant was meaningless or, even worse, something negative that you had to overcome. However genuinely fulfilled you feel by your observant life, you must take great care not to communicate, even unwittingly, to your parents that your "real" life began only when you became observant. It may well have been launched in a new direction at that time, but your life began in your parents' home, and your parents' influence has had and will continue to have an impact on the person you have become. And they still have important things to teach you.

BUT HOW DO I KNOW THAT YOU ARE THINKING CLEARLY ENOUGH TO MAKE SUCH A HUGE DECISION?

Although most parents would not use such a strong word, when they try to imagine what it means to be part of an observant community, the word "cult" will come to mind for some, along with certain stereotypes. If this is how they are feeling about your religious choices, they can't possibly embrace any potential marriage partner you would bring them. If they see you as having been brainwashed by your rabbi or community, your choice of partner can't be a clearheaded decision, right? Again, let's view this through your parents' eyes and figure out how to allay their fears.

From their point of view, there's now a rabbi and a community in your life advising you on how to live every aspect of it—how to dress, what to eat, which schools to attend, whom to marry. They are afraid that you have become unable to think for yourself, that you are a manifestation of the people who have "programmed" you, and that now, at such a young age, you've been brainwashed into marrying someone else who is not able to think clearly. Sounds like a setup for failure, doesn't it? (Interestingly, the divorce rate among Orthodox Jews is much lower than the national average. But for the most part, divorce is not discouraged. It is viewed as a halachically sanctioned way to end a marriage that has not worked out.)

Here's how you can reassure worried family members that you haven't joined a cult. Being a member of a cult implies an allegiance to a religious doctrine or to a leader that is based not on intellectual conviction, but, rather, on emotional fervor. It is only when someone is swept away emotionally and unable to employ logic or common sense to objectively evaluate the belief system of which he is a part that we would call that person brainwashed, or part of a cult.

The most important point you can make to your parents is one that we have already discussed in the kashrus chapter: You don't believe and behave as you do because some charismatic, cultic figure has convinced you to do so. Observant Judaism is based on one historic, defining event: the revelation on Mount Sinai as recorded in the Torah and as transmitted to succeeding generations by the men and women who personally witnessed it. Historians believe that the Trojan War occurred because they read contemporaneous accounts of it that have been handed down over the centuries. And even if there are no documents available that "prove" it, an African American living in New York today knows that his great-great-grandfather was a slave in Mississippi in the 1850s because his grandfather told him so, and his grandfather knows it because he heard it from his grandfather, who was the slave.

Jews have believed for thousands of years that when we

study the Torah and the Oral Law we are studying the word of God as transmitted to Moses, who transmitted this to the Israelites in the desert, who transmitted it to succeeding generations, and that this continued until these oral laws were written down hundreds of years later. Observant Judaism is not based on blind faith. It is based on knowledge.

Your parents may fear that you have been swept away emotionally and that your ability to make intellectually sound decisions has been compromised, so they need to be reassured that as an observant Jew your approach to God is not through the emotional path of faith, but through the intellectual path of knowledge. One of the first things we teach our children is to ask the four questions at the Passover Seder. The first verse of the Shema deals with the knowledge of God; it is then followed by the obligation to love God. All newly observant Jews are encouraged to study the Torah so that they can understand rationally, not emotionally, the basis for the laws we are required to follow, so that they can understand the essential truth contained within the Torah. You did not make a serious commitment to be observant only because you were attracted to, for example, the beauty of Shabbos and the warmth of Jewish family life.

Lest your parents be concerned about the other extreme—an intellectual obsession with truth but, God forbid, no feeling in your heart—you can explain to them how you feel when you look at the Shabbos candles on the table on Friday night or when you celebrate the Torah-reading cycle on Simchas Torah. And if your parents are worried that you aren't mature enough to make a decision as major as becoming observant (and getting married at such a young age!), perhaps you can help them see this irony: The fact that you have decided to be observant in a time and place when it would be so much easier to not be is the single greatest piece of evidence that you are capable of independent thinking! You must have acquired a certain level of confidence and self-respect to have the courage and conviction to turn away from a great deal of secular culture to live as an observant Jew.

Who says my son or daughter is an independent thinker, your parents might say. He calls his rabbi for everything! Let's take a look at this concern and help you reassure your parents about this important relationship in your life.

LET'S TALK ABOUT THE RABBI

You probably have a rabbi—or more than one rabbi—who has been closely involved in helping you decide to become observant; whose school you may have attended; whose weekend retreats you may still attend; with whom you may still study; whom you call when you have questions about laws, customs, rituals, and the theology of observance. He probably plays a big role in your life. But what is important to convey to your parents is that your rabbi is a teacher—a scholar who is explicating Jewish law, history, philosophy, and theology, all of it *text-based.* His role is to clarify what the Torah, the Talmud, and the many commentaries and codes of law have to say about how observant Jews should live their lives. A rabbi's words are valued only to the extent that he can show that he is essentially quoting from the

Torah. And even that limited power is further limited by the fact that the rabbi can't just say, "This is what the Torah teaches us." He has to demonstrate how what he is saying is deduced or derived from the Torah. Any original insight that a rabbi may offer is subject to intense collegial scrutiny to determine if it is a legitimate deduction from the Torah. Instead of feeling that you are swallowing everything your rabbis have taught you without any thought or debate, your parents might be surprised to discover how much debate and argument occurs inside a yeshivah!

Is there an emotional component to how you feel about your rabbi? Of course there is. Helen Keller loved her teacher, Anne Sullivan. Her parents understood where that love came from. If you explain it to your parents the right way, hopefully they will understand how you feel about your rabbi and other beloved teachers.

BUT I'M WORRIED THAT MY CHILD IS NO LONGER NORMAL

First you became observant. Then you didn't continue down the career path your parents had expected you to follow. Now you want to get married in your early twenties, something no one does anymore—at least no one in your parents' circle. You also seem to be so serious all the time. To your parents you don't appear to be "normal" anymore, and this worries them.

While normal is a very subjective word, all parents want to be reassured that their child is normal. What we need to figure out is, What does "normal" mean? If "normal" means that your mind is healthy, that you are psychologically stable, that all of your faculties and senses are working, and that your inclinations to love and be loved are as powerful as those of any other human being, then you are normal! If, on the other hand, "normal" means "my child accepts and has adopted the values of contemporary secular society," then it's true, as a newly observant Jew you are striving to be anything but normal. You intentionally do not participate in many activities that most people nowadays think of as normal. Hopefully, your parents will eventually understand why you feel this way. But for the short term, what they want is reassurance about the simple, everyday things that are part of how you now live your life: Do you still try to sneak over the speed limit when you're in a rush? Do you still root for your favorite baseball team? Do you still care if the person you marry is nice-looking? Do you still eat junk food, drink cappuccinos, and laugh with your friends? Do we have to worry about your having any fun in your life?

With some effort on your part, you should be able to reassure your parents that by becoming observant you have not lost your capacity to enjoy life. Although the way you enjoy life may be different than the way the contemporary secular world enjoys life, your basic human nature is the same as it was before you became observant. You are, indeed, still "normal" enough for your parents to be able to relate to, and to be proud of.

Now that we have discussed some of the fears your parents might have that would keep them from feeling they can evaluate in any helpful way your choice of mate, we also need to deal with another problem you may encounter with them. Let's face it, observant dating practices are, to most people, just plain weird, and they're certainly hopelessly outdated. You could be setting yourself up to make a terrible mistake that will wreck the rest of your life. At least that's how they see it.

YOU CALL THIS DATING?

Even though contemporary dating practices and teenage and young adult relationships can be a source of considerable worry for parents, at least these problems are familiar and understandable to them. Aside from seeing how arranged marriages are portrayed in *Fiddler on the Roof* or described in novels, most people have no idea how observant Jews meet, date, and marry. And what they think they know about it, they don't like. However well you succeed in clarifying the virtues of the "mind before heart" approach to dating, your parents will still wonder when—and if—romance ever enters into it. This mind-set generally comes from the world of arranged marriages as it is portrayed in, for example, *Fiddler on the Roof,* where the matchmaker's main concern is how rich or poor everyone involved is, and the daughters who marry men they have met on their own and fallen in love with are depicted as courageous women who are helping to destroy an archaic system that made everyone involved miserable. The reality of matchmaking and networking in the observant world today as a way for compatible men and women to meet each other is a far cry from the world of Tevye and his daughters. Anyone who has seen a starry-eyed young observant couple on their wedding day knows that these people are very much in love. How do observant dating practices promote and encourage falling in love, even though the men and women know each other for only a few months before they marry, and have no physical contact with each other during that time? This is something you will have to explain to your family. Here's how.

We've all seen the statistics: As a society, we are choosing to marry later and later. In America, more people than ever before are in their late twenties to early thirties at the time of their first marriage. They want to complete their education, begin to establish careers, satisfy youthful wanderlust, and figure out who they are before they decide with whom they are, hopefully, going to spend the rest of their lives. A series of "relationships" supplies emotional and physical companionship, may lead to something more permanent, and even if it doesn't, it's a good "learning experience" for an eventual permanent relationship. Even if your parents married in their twenties and are still happily married many years later, they probably feel that times have changed since they were young. But they might also be worried about today's divorce statistics, and they might well be open to appreciating the value in a new—or, more accurately, old—approach to dating and marriage. On the other hand, even if they aren't convinced that the modern way of dating, living together, and then getting married is the way to go, when faced with the other extreme, you could very well hear the following.

YOU'VE BEEN GOING OUT WITH HIM FOR ONLY THREE MONTHS! HOW CAN YOU BE SURE THAT HE'S THE RIGHT ONE?

Rodgers and Hammerstein weren't wrong: "You may see a stranger across a crowded room / And somehow you know, you know even then . . ." No one can explain why two people are attracted to each other. Not even observant Jews, who try to explain almost everything. It just happens, and usually both parties know it fairly quickly into a dating relationship. But there is, of course, much more to establishing a permanent relationship than that. When observant Jews date, both parties understand that it is for one purpose and one purpose only: to evaluate whether or not the person you are with is a potential spouse. This is, on some level, what most people think about when they date—some of the time, anyway. But when observant Jews date, it is what both the man and the woman are thinking about, first and foremost and all of the time, and they both know it. They know within the first few dates, sometimes within the first hour or so, whether or not they are attracted to each other. And they can fairly quickly figure out whether their personal goals, interests, religious philosophy, family and friends, politics, and feelings about eventually settling in Israel, among other life issues, mesh. If you are a career woman who seeks a business-oriented guy, you aren't going to spend time with a man who has made it clear to those who know him that he's looking for a woman who will be a full-time mom. Likewise, if you are a guy who wants to spend a few years learning Torah full-time before embarking on your career, you aren't going to spend time with a woman who would be turned off by this idea.

Observant couples don't go to movies or have physical contact while they are dating; the time they spend together is focused on one goal—determining whether or not they are personally and intellectually compatible. What dating couples basically do is talk, talk, and talk. Your parents would be amazed at how much a couple can learn about each other in a short amount of time if all they do is talk to each other.

WITH ALL THIS TALKING, DO YOU REALLY FALL IN LOVE?

As we discussed in the chapter on modesty, in most observant circles single young men and women have very little social contact with one another, so they rely on friends, family, teachers, etc., to introduce them to eligible fellow singles. You don't want to hope for a stroke of luck—that you encounter "the one" as he or she is leaving the supermarket. It could happen, but let's not count on it.

One way that this "fix up" type of dating differs from the more conventional boy-meets-girl dating that your parents are familiar with is in all the preparation that goes on before the guy and the girl actually meet. The person who is fixing you up knows you and knows what you are looking for in a mate and also knows, directly or indirectly, the person you are being fixed up with. In addition, it's perfectly acceptable (it's actually recommended) for you to ask third parties who are acquainted with both of you if they think the two of you are a match on the most basic level. Dating isn't viewed as entertainment; it's a responsibility, and you want to do it efficiently so that time isn't wasted or people's feelings hurt. Contemporary secular culture tells us that falling in love happens spontaneously, when two people spend time together and enjoy each other's company. What you can explain to your parents is that when you've decided—with your head—what you are looking for in a mate, and you have elected to meet only people who have a good chance of meeting those criteria, this actually encourages you to fall in love—with your heart—with the right person once you've found him. You aren't going into a date cold, knowing nothing about this person. You've talked with people who know him and have spoken highly of him. And he's done the same thing on his end. When you do finally meet, you already know a great deal about each other and you both like what you know, so you approach this meeting with open hearts and open minds. You're not afraid to fall in love with this person because you may discover down the road that your life goals are incompatible. You already know that you have a lot in common. So if the chemistry is there, let the falling-in-love process begin. If it's not there, you'll know it pretty quickly, perhaps after a date or two, and the relationship will end. What observant Jews don't do is date for months, decide to try living together, develop emotional attachments, and then painfully end the relationship when they decide they are incompatible.

Your family may be intrigued by the observant view that

falling in the kind of love that leads to a successful marriage is actually easier when you will only date someone with whom you already know you have a lot in common, as opposed to someone with whom you simply have an instant physical attraction. And given that they are now looking at things from an "older and wiser" perspective, they might well admit that getting physically involved quickly often produces the opposite of true intimacy. Although an observant couple will not even so much as hold hands, when they fall in love they look and feel much like any other couple in the first blush of love.

BUT WHY DOES IT HAVE TO BE DONE SO FAST?

Even if your parents can be convinced that the Orthodox dating process works and that it might well be the best way for you to find your ideal mate, don't be surprised if they still want to slow you down in the rush to date and get married. They understand that once you begin dating, marriage is probably not far away. In fact, once you've fallen in love with someone, since you will not be having physical contact with that person until after you are married, you're pretty eager to move things along to the wedding day—usually within three to six months of becoming engaged. Celibacy before marriage is a given for observant Jews, and observant Jews may be disciplined about not getting sexually involved before marriage, but they are human and they have the same urges as anyone else—especially when they fall in love!

A long engagement puts great stress on a couple who can't be intimate with each other until their wedding night. Yes, your mother will probably not be happy about the fact that she's got three months to plan your wedding, but it gets done all the time—and quite beautifully, too. Things will go a lot smoother when she comes to realize that you really are in love; that your intended is a wonderful person, a true mensch; and that you aren't passing up opportunities to find someone better.

AND WHAT ABOUT MONEY?

Your parents know that most observant Jews begin having a family as soon as they are married. They are concerned—and rightly so—that because of all the expenses associated with raising a family, you will deny yourself important opportunities for career advancement or just to have fun before you have to start saving money for tuition, summer camp, and orthodontia. They may even be worried that you will expect them to support you financially until your careers are established. Although this is frequently the case in the observant world, if your parents are not observant, you can't assume that they will be open to the idea of supporting you and your young family so that their son can study Torah or so that the two of you can finish your college education. It would be the rare family, indeed, that would be so supportive of your decision to become observant that they would generously agree to support you as newlyweds as well. Unless your parents have already told you that they are able and willing to help you out, you and your fiancé will have to put together your own plan for supporting yourselves, and you will have to reassure your parents that they aren't written into the plan, unless they want to be!

Looking at the world from your parents' point of view—yes, having children when you are young will saddle you with responsibilities that most people your age don't have. So you will want to help them see this from your perspective. For observant Jews, marrying and raising children is the most important part of God's plan for us on earth. The Torah tells us that the first commandment God gave to Adam and Eve was not "observe the Sabbath" or "keep kosher," but "be fruitful and multiply." Yes, it's important to do whatever you can to support your family properly, but having children when you are young doesn't mean you will wreck your chances for career advancement; it just means that it may take more effort on your part. For observant Jews, the primary obligation is finding the person you will be spending the rest of your life with and, once you have found that person, beginning to build a beautiful Jewish home together. There is no greater joy than that. To young observant Jews considering marriage before a career is fully established, a spouse and children are not entanglements that will get in the way of that career, but, rather, a constant reminder of what they are working for. It's not the moment when the check gets deposited into the bank that they dream about, but the sight of a child's smile when they arrive home from work.

YOU AND YOUR PARENTS WANT THE SAME THING

Both you and your parents want you to find a wonderful person with whom you will share a long and happy life. Your parents want to love this person and welcome him or her into your family, and they are excited about the prospect of becoming grandparents—sooner rather than later if you marry young! But, as with everything regarding the way you have chosen to live your religious life, you are first going to have to do some preparatory work with your family, so that they understand where you are coming from and what your religious beliefs have to do with how you go about finding your spouse. If your parents express curiosity about the details of matchmaking and shidduchim, and they want a better understanding of how you meet the people you date or how you met the person you are presenting to them as your beloved, share with them the details and include them in this important chapter in your life. If you explain it to them properly, you will have helped to create an atmosphere of love and acceptance when you introduce your mom and dad to the most important person in your life.

If your parents feel that you couldn't possibly be in love and ready to get married after such a short period of acquaintance, don't be shy about sharing your excitement and anticipation with them, and sharing with them your feelings about your fiancée. When you share your joy with your parents, when they see the way you can't stop smiling whenever you talk about her, they'll remember how they felt when they first fell in love. Observant or nonobservant, falling in love is still falling in love.

ON A PERSONAL NOTE

Stephen and I do not have fond memories of our teenage dating experiences, or of our adult forays into the singles' scene. I didn't marry Stephen until I was thirty-three—after way too many dates and boyfriends. Stephen was married and divorced before he met me. High on the list of reasons we decided to raise our children as observant Jews from birth was our desire to spare them from this pain! Do people with whom we were friendly before we became observant think that the Orthodox dating system is a bit strange? Yes, they probably do. But at this point in our lives, Stephen and I think that the way we used to live our lives is a lot stranger, and we are grateful to be offering our children an alternative.

Five

WHAT DO YOU MEAN, YOU CAN'T COME TO YOUR SISTER'S WEDDING?

How to Participate in Family Life-Cycle Events

Family simchas celebrate milestones in the lives of its members. Families that are dispersed across the continent, and sometimes across the world, will often put great personal effort and expense into being present at these gatherings. Weddings, circumcisions, bar or bat mitzvahs, birthday and anniversary celebrations, and, regrettably, funerals are generally regarded as events not to be missed for any reason other than illness or disability. For some families, it is only at these events that cousins, aunts, uncles, and even siblings have an opportunity to see one another. As families grow and multiply, spreading out all over the world, simchas are the ropes that pull the disparate parts of the family back to a place where, once again, they are all connected.

Unfortunately, religious differences can become particularly divisive elements during the celebration of a simchah. When an observant Jew is invited to the simchah of a non- or less-observant relative, or vice versa, dozens of practical questions arise as soon as the invitations show up in the mail. Matters of concern for the observant family member might include:

- Can I attend the event if the food served is not kosher?
- Can I attend if there will be social dancing?
- Can I attend if a microphone is used during a Shabbos synagogue service? Or if there is no mechitzah, and men and women sit together in the synagogue?
- What should I do if many of the women attending will be immodestly dressed?

Less- or nonobservant Jews invited to the simchah of a more observant relative will have their own concerns:

- Will I have to wear a long-sleeved, high-necked blouse and below-the-knee skirt?
- Will they expect me to cover my head with a hat, or even worse?
- Isn't the service all in Hebrew and three hours long?
- Do I really have to sit apart from my husband, and behind a divider? What's the point of going if I can't even see or hear what's going on?

To be perfectly honest, these practical concerns are easier to deal with than ideological issues, but there is plenty of opportunity for peaceful resolution to all of them.

IDEOLOGICAL CONFLICT

I'll address the practical issues later on, but it's important first to understand the ideology behind the answers to these questions, and to take a deeper look at the source of the pain that arises when a family member chooses not to attend a simchah because of religious or ideological concerns. If you understand better how to articulate your reasons for not attending, you can perhaps appease your angry or hurt relatives. Here's a way to think about it, and to communicate it to them.

Let's look at a very common scenario: an intermarriage that is presided over by both a rabbi and non-Jewish clergy, or by only a rabbi. The position of the observant Jew is that this is not something he is allowed to attend because intermarriage is not something he can celebrate. However well intentioned the motivation may be, providing kosher food will not help; intermarriage, according to observant Jews, violates one of the core principles of Jewish law and the continuity of the Jewish people. If this happens in your family, you will just have to explain, as politely and compassionately as you can, that although you may still love the bride or the groom, you simply cannot attend the wedding.

It works both ways. Your relatives may decide not to attend one of your simchas because it in some way violates their ideological principles. For example, there are people who will not pray in a synagogue that seats women separately, behind a wall or a curtain, or in a synagogue that doesn't count women as part of a minyan because they feel this is discriminatory.

Less-observant family members hosting a simchah will often feel hurt and rejected if you tell them you can't attend their simchah because of religious or ideological issues. These feelings are articulated, or at least felt, as two distinct accusations:

- How could your religion and ideology be more important to you than your own family?
- Do you think you are better than we are because you are more observant than we are?

These two questions go to the heart of much of the conflict that may occur between you and your family; there is almost no issue discussed in this book that doesn't derive from these feelings.

How could your religion and ideology be more important to you than your own family?

Staying true to your religious beliefs and ideology and being devoted to your family are both admirable qualities. But when they come into conflict, how do you choose?

The knee-jerk reaction to this question is usually "Of course, family comes first!" But there are times when this is not necessarily so. During the Civil War there were many instances of families where one son, living in the South, enlisted in the Confederate Army and another son, living in the North, enlisted the Union Army, even though they knew they might encounter each other on the battlefield. Or, for a more contemporary example, when Senator Edward Kennedy addressed the Democratic National Convention in the summer of 2004, a whole bunch of Kennedy cousins were in the VIP boxes, including niece Maria Shriver but not including her husband, Republican Governor Arnold Schwarzenegger. And when Governor Schwarzenegger addressed the Republican National Convention later that summer, there was Maria sitting in the VIP box, but there were no other Kennedys there, and she didn't go down to the podium and wave to the crowd with him when he was finished, like the spouses of all the other speakers.

When staying true to your religious beliefs means that you cannot participate in a family event, it doesn't mean you don't love and respect your family, and it's your responsibility to communicate this to them in a way they will understand. We've discussed in previous chapters why, because you believe in the divine origin of your belief system, you can't just "bend a little every once in a while." Your relatives may not be religious, but they certainly have ideological principles, and this might be one way to help them understand why you feel as you do.

The fact that Marsha, an ardent feminist, will not attend her brother's simchah because she is angry about the mechitzah and what she feels it represents does not reflect a lack of love for her brother. Because of her love for him, she will probably agonize over how to tell him that she cannot come. Her brother might think she's wrong and he may feel compelled to explain to her why the mechitzah is not what she thinks it is. But rather than feeling rejected, he can be admiring of his sister's commitment to her ideals. Even though she loves her family, for her the rights of women are a larger concern.

For the observant Jew who loves his family, God's commandments and his responsibility as a member of the observant Jewish community must come before his personal devotion to his family. For religious and ideological reasons, he, too, might not be able to attend a family simchah.

Do you think you are better than we are because you are more observant than we are?

Now we've come to the primary source for a lot of tension and bad feeling between newly observant Jews and their less- or nonobservant relatives. If there is one accusation that, more than any other, is directed by less-observant relatives toward more observant family members, it is that because you have taken on so many more religious obligations and responsibilities than those with which you were raised, you now feel that you are better than everyone else in your family. Whether this is actually articulated by your relatives or just a sentiment that you feel floating around in the air whenever you get together with your family, this feeling can destroy any possibility of your being able to spend enjoyable time together with your relatives.

Whether it's using your Hebrew name instead of the English name your parents gave you, or deciding to keep kosher, dress more modestly, observe Shabbos and holidays more strictly, or leave your family's synagogue and join a new one—whatever change you make in the way you live your life might well be perceived by your family as meaning that you are looking down on them for the way they live their lives. You may indeed, in your heart of hearts, wish that they led more observant lives. But that doesn't mean you look down on them because they don't. However, your family may feel, simply because of your actions, that you do. In a world where people crave respect and dignity, feeling "not good enough" is one of the most painful experiences a human being can know.

Your relatives might think that you believe you are "better" than they are because of your religious observance. Let's dissect this word, "better," a relative term if ever there was one. New York Yankee fans will swear that their Yankees are "better" than the Boston Red Sox (and vice versa). Coca-Cola fans will insist that Coke is "better" than Pepsi. There are Web sites devoted to discussions of who is "better"—Captain James T. Kirk or Captain Jean-Luc Picard. Who is a "better" driver? The cautious one who won't drive over 65 miles per hour, or the hot rodder who can keep a car on the road at over 120 miles per hour? Who defines "better," and according to what criteria? Is being better the same thing as being right?

To understand what is and is not meant by "better," we need to identify two separate struggles—between right and wrong, and between good and bad. The attempt to lead a moral life is a two-step process. First come the intellectual and philosophical questions: "What do I believe is the moral way to live my life? How does religion enter into it, if at all? If I believe in God, how do I know how God wants me to live my life?" When you've figured this out, you've established your moral code, your standards for what you believe is "right" and "wrong."

The second stage is more of an emotional struggle than a philosophical rumination. Once you've determined what the right way for you to live your life is, how do you go about living up to those standards? And what happens if you don't? Does that make you "bad"?

An adult child who is careful about seeing to the needs of his elderly parents is generally regarded as someone who is doing the "right" thing. But is someone who calls his parents every day a "better" son than someone who calls his parents once a week? By no means can we make such an objective evaluation of a very subjective experience. Perhaps the son who calls every day is "better" at keeping in touch with his parents by phone, but he visits them only once a year, whereas the son who is in touch infrequently by phone visits his parents every other Shabbos. Who is considered the "better" son? This is too subjective a situation for us to say.

Back to our question: So, do you think you are better than we are?

The observant Jew believes she is living her life the way God wants all Jews to live their lives. She does believe that what she is doing is right. But does this mean that she thinks she is a better human being than her nonobservant relatives? No. She may feel that if her relatives had accompanied her on her religious quest, they would have come to the same conclusions that she did and would have become observant themselves. But the fact that they have not does not make them bad people.

Do observant Jews believe in religious truths and in a right way to observe God's laws? Yes. Are people who do not observe in this way "bad" people? No. Many newly observant Jews are very proud of a nurturing sister who helps troubled youth as a social worker, a studious nephew who took first prize at a science fair, or a compassionate mother who volunteers at the synagogue more hours than anyone can count. Even if they believe that their religious views are the right ones, observant Jews understand that theological arguments about whether or not God gave us the Torah and what this means for us are debates between the right and wrong ways to understand the Torah, and not debates between "good" and "bad" people. So, the answer to the question "Do you believe you are better than we are?" is no. We believe we are right when it comes to Torah observance, but that doesn't make us "better" than any other Jew.

UNDERSTANDING WHERE YOUR RELATIVES ARE COMING FROM

As careful as you are about not appearing judgmental to your nonobservant relatives, you may still encounter resentment and hostility from them. Why? Until the eighteenth century most Jews maintained pretty much the same level of religious belief and observance. There were theological differences of opinion between the rabbis of the Talmudic era and the rabbis of the Middle Ages, but the fundamental, core beliefs were shared by all. However, during the period referred to as the Haskalah, or Enlightenment, different philosophies about the existence of God, the accuracy of the Bible, and the importance, or even validity, of religious faith and practice were advanced, and they were accepted by Jews throughout the world. These beliefs were diametrically opposed to traditional Jewish theology. Observant Jews from that time on have believed that these beliefs are heretical.

There are many Jews today who feel that the secular, humanistic approach to Judaism is the way to go, and they may think that traditionally observant Jews are rigid and misguided. Some of your relatives might be affiliated with what are known as other "denominations" or "streams" of Judaism. Their belief systems include making concessions or accommodations for modernity and secular life that traditionally observant Jews do not agree with. You can, they feel, be a believing Jew and a "modern" twenty-first-century American, and these two ways of living don't have to conflict. You can have the best of both worlds, so to speak.

But then along comes a son who, after having been raised in a more modern belief system, decides to journey back three hundred years, returning to a theology that his family feels is outdated. He no longer wants to deviate from what he has come to understand is the original, correct way to be observant—the way God explained it to

Moses on Mount Sinai and the way Moses then explained it to the Children of Israel. He will no longer be able to participate in quite the same way at his parents' annual Labor Day barbecue because he's now following the Torah's laws, and eating barbecued Perdue chicken is just not part of them.

It doesn't matter if you never, ever, say to your relatives "It's wrong for you to eat that nonkosher chicken." There will be tension at the barbecue whether or not this is said. Your family might feel resentful that, by not eating their chicken, you are making an issue out of it. Some who are ambivalent about their own level of observance, or lack of it, might feel guilty about eating nonkosher food in front of you. How will they deal with this emotional tumult? They could project those feelings back on you, either accusing you of looking down on them because they don't observe Judaism the way you do, or attempting to convince you that it's you who are wrong for refusing to accept that modern times call for flexibility and a more open mind. And they'll most likely mention that family harmony should always come first.

Some of your relatives may be very comfortable with their chosen level of observance, and they will be able to more easily adopt a "live and let live" attitude toward this whole topic. Sometimes, though, you will encounter a relative who is personally wrestling with his conscience about whether his coaching soccer on Saturdays, eating in nonkosher restaurants, and working on many of the Jewish holidays are really okay things for him to do as a Jew. Then you may well encounter even more hostility, and the "So, you think you're better than us?" question. You've sparked the discomfort in them, but much of this isn't about you at all. You are reflecting back to them their own internal turmoil.

What can you do about this? Unfortunately, not all that much. Engaging in theological debate with your relatives will only make them angrier. Even anything that *sounds* like you're trying to convince them to take on some of your religious practices will probably backfire. All you can do is reinforce how important it is for you to continue to be a part of your family, without compromising your commitment to Torah, and to demonstrate this whenever and wherever possible.

WHAT TO DO—OR WHAT NOT TO DO— WHEN YOU ARE INVITED TO A SIMCHAH HOSTED BY A LESS-OBSERVANT RELATIVE

Most of the religious questions that come up can be answered by keeping the following in mind:

> The Torah requires you to observe the positive laws, i.e., the "thou shalts," and to refrain from breaking or causing another Jew to break the negative laws, i.e., the "thou shalt nots." However, it does not usually prohibit you from being present in a situation where other Jews are not observing Jewish law.

With this principle in mind, you will probably be able to attend more family simchas than you thought you could. Even if the simchah is not being celebrated in full accordance with Jewish law (for example, nonkosher food is being served), if you yourself are not violating Jewish law at this simchah, you can attend some, most, or even all of it. Everyone else getting up to fox-trot or boogie? Go over and catch up with Great-uncle Murray, whose dancing days are long past. Are there some women dressed less than modestly? Just do what you do on the train; find something else to look at. Your hosts may ask you in advance if they can order a kosher meal for you, so you can eat along with everyone else. Needless to say, you should express appropriate gratitude for their thoughtfulness, but you will need to make sure that the meal is certified kosher by a reputable kosher-certifying agency and not simply kosher-style or vegetarian. The meal should come to your table sealed in plastic or tinfoil, with the seal of the kosher-certifying agency prominently displayed on the front. The waiter may ask you if it's okay for the meal to be heated; it is, so long as it's sealed while it's being heated. To be honest, these meals do vary in quality, depending on whether they come from one of those companies that supplies kosher food for airlines or from a local kosher caterer that supplies individual meals as part of a service to nonkosher caterers. Who among us hasn't tasted that delicacy "airline chicken"? Yum. But whether its rubber chicken or fresh prime rib, remember to thank your host for it when you say your goodbyes. You aren't attending for the food, anyway.

ON A PERSONAL NOTE

I once attended a catered family event in a town that had a kosher caterer. The host of the event, my aunt, was kind enough to bring in a kosher meal for me from the kosher caterer, and she was even sensitive enough to serve me a meal that was similar to that which every one else was eating so I didn't stand out with a big neon sign that read SHE WON'T EAT OUR FOOD! The food was delicious, far better than the dreaded airplane chicken. If there is a kosher caterer in town, this option can work quite well, and for only a small extra expense on the part of the host.

SHALL WE DANCE?

For a simchah with a sizable percentage of observant guests, your host might even go to the trouble of ensuring your participation by setting aside small corner areas on the dance floor where men and women can dance in separate circles. If you are a woman who won't dance without a partition, perhaps you can find a small room off to the side in which to dance. If the lead singer in the band is a woman, an observant man should quietly step into the hallway while she is singing—again, this is a good opportunity to catch up with other nondancing relatives—and return when the singing has stopped. There are observant Jews who rarely leave home without a sefer—a Bible, a book of the Talmud, or a book of Jewish law—which they will take out and study during periods of time when they are otherwise unoccupied (on the train, for instance). If you excuse yourself and go to the lobby to study during the female singer's performance, your relatives may find this a bit odd, so you'll want to explain it to them; once you've done so, it won't be an issue. But avoid opening up a sefer at the table, when your relatives are expecting you to engage in conversation!

One possibly problematic aspect of attending a simchah hosted by less-observant relatives is the feasibility of bringing along your children. They will be taken aback by the social dancing and strapless minidresses, and you'll need to explain to them why they can't go over to the buffet tables and take whatever they want. But as far as young children are concerned, as long as you've brought along food they can eat and they have plenty of little cousins to run around with, they will be fine. You may feel that you don't want your older children to attend because of the dancing and the way some of the guests are dressed. Some observant families feel more strongly than others about insulating their children from the less-observant world around them. These decisions are individual and personal in nature, but you should in any case consult your rabbi, especially if your parents will be hurt if your children aren't there.

If you have explained your situation to your relatives the right way, your decision to attend the simchah even if you don't fully participate in all of its activities will elicit a positive reaction—"We must be really important to them; even though they can't eat or dance, they still want to be here!"—and not a negative one—"Why aren't they eating or dancing at my wedding?" Your hosts might wish to encourage your attendance and involvement by providing a mechitzah for separate dancing by men and women for at least part of the time, or by hiring a band whose lead singer is a man. But if they aren't willing or able to offer these concessions, or if it would make them too uncomfortable to do so because other relatives in attendance would have a negative reaction to their doing so, don't make an issue out of it. This is their simchah, not yours. You are an invited guest, and this isn't the time to preach about why men and women dancing together is not something you, or the Torah, deem acceptable.

WHAT TO DO WHEN YOU CAN'T ATTEND

There are times when the circumstances are such that it's best not to attend a family simchah even though, technically, you are permitted to do so and even though your family may be upset. Sometimes, even though you have made many allowable concessions to attend the simchah, what will stick out more than anything are the ways in which you are not able to participate, and what people will remember most is the tension that this created for everyone.

As one Jewish man said to me about his observant sister's decision not to attend his daughter's weekend bat mitzvah, "I told my sister it would probably be better if she didn't come. She wouldn't be able to join us for Friday night activities at my home because we aren't within walking distance of the synagogue, and she would be staying at some stranger's house that is within walking distance of the synagogue. She couldn't be in any of the family pictures taken on the Sabbath. She wouldn't witness the actual ceremony in the sanctuary because it's in a Reform temple, which she doesn't go into, and she couldn't eat anything at the afternoon lunch. It didn't make a lot of sense for her to come such a distance when she really couldn't participate in most of the event. I felt that I, and others, would notice her absence and lack of participation more than her presence, and it wouldn't feel like she was really celebrating with us."

In this case, the brother didn't resent his sister's nonattendance because she *was* willing to come, despite the inconvenience and all the parts of the event that she'd have to sit out. It was he who, after giving it some thought, let her know that it was okay for her not to attend. The message his sister therefore communicated to her family was not "I don't care about you, and that's why I'm not coming," but, rather, "We both agree that logically it doesn't make a lot of sense for me to come such a distance when I'd have to skip out on almost all of the event." This woman was fortunate to have a very understanding brother. But no matter how understanding your family is, there are times when they will feel hurt because you will not be able to participate in some aspects of their simchah because of religious restrictions. It's your responsibility to explain as sensitively as possible what you can and can't do and, if possible, why.

A sore point with your family is certain to be the fact that Orthodox Jews cannot daven in non-Orthodox synagogues. They can understand the rule about not entering a church, but another synagogue? We're all Jews, aren't we!

One problem is the lack of a mechitzah—the partition or curtain that separates the men from the women during prayer. But even if your host would be willing to make an accommodation for separate, curtained-off areas for Orthodox men and women within the sanctuary, that wouldn't entirely solve the problem. Most Orthodox rabbinical authorities hold that davening in the synagogue of a different denomination—a denomination whose theology is at variance with Orthodox theology on so many core issues—is not allowed. Doing so gives an unspoken assent to the denial of Jewish law and practice that have been officially sanctioned by these denominations, and an observant Jew is not allowed even to appear to lend his endorsement to any Jewish belief system that rejects the divine origin of Torah. There are those who would argue that mere attendance does not imply endorsement, but that's just not the case. Attendance, or lack of it, makes a very loud statement.

For a weekend bar or bat mitzvah, one option might be davening at a nearby Orthodox synagogue and, so long as you are able to get kosher food, joining your family for Friday night dinner and Shabbos afternoon lunch. Can you attend a wedding ceremony being performed in the sanctuary of a non-Orthodox denomination? There are different rabbinic opinions; ask your rabbi. And what about attending a wedding performed on Shabbos? Jewish law prohibits weddings on Shabbos and Jewish holidays because parts of the wedding involve business transactions, and, as we discussed in the chapter on Shabbos and Jewish holidays, Jews are not allowed to conduct business on those days. So if your nephew is getting married on Shabbos or on a Jewish holiday, even if the wedding is being held at a hall that is within walking distance, you probably can't attend. Ask your rabbi if there's any sort of concession that can be made, but the answer may well be no. This will be a tough one to explain to your relatives, who are thinking, "What's the problem? It's a Jewish wedding that's being presided over by a rabbi!" Hopefully, through reading this book you will have the tools to explain the situation to your family in a way they can understand and accept, even if they won't be happy about it.

GENERAL GUIDELINES FOR NON- OR LESS-OBSERVANT RELATIVES INVITED TO YOUR SIMCHAH

When it's you who are making the simchah, your relatives will have a few significant concerns:

- Will I unintentionally do something to embarrass myself in front of all these religious people?
- Will I unintentionally do something to embarrass my religious relatives in front of their friends?
- Do I have to conduct myself religiously the way all these people are doing, even though I don't ordinarily do so?

These are all perfectly legitimate questions, and it is your responsibility to make your relatives feel comfortable at your simchah.

Some hosts will prepare photocopied booklets that explain

what transpires at an observant wedding. They can be put near the place cards. Your relatives will be grateful to have them, as they will answer many of the questions they have, and it shows that you have made a special effort for them to feel included. Yarmulkes can also be placed near the place cards. Most of your relatives will appreciate this gesture, too, and will put them on. You will have put little booklets containing the Grace After Meals on all the tables. If your relatives pick them up and say the Grace along with everyone else, that's great; if they don't, that's okay, too.

Many of your relatives will know that low-cut dresses, bare shoulders, miniskirts, and skirts slit up the thigh are not appropriate attire for an observant wedding. Some may even ask you in advance what is and is not appropriate to wear. But some of your relatives won't have a clue. If you think it would be a good idea to discuss this with them beforehand, you can call them before the simchah and say something like, "I don't want you to think you've got to buy a whole new wardrobe for Chaim's bar mitzvah—anything modest and conservative would be appropriate, and I'm sure you've already got something in your closet that would be fine. Can I give you a few suggestions on what you might want to avoid?"

The most thoughtful thing you can do for relatives who come to your synagogue and have no idea what is going on is to pair them with a friend or family member who will sit next to them and offer to help them navigate the prayer book. This will be greatly appreciated. If they have shown up, they want to participate just like everyone else.

WHAT ABOUT THE RELATIVES WHO JUST DON'T GO FOR ANY OF THIS?

Uncle Harry has always thought that wearing a kippah and a prayer shawl in synagogue is completely unnecessary. Aunt Gladys has never sat behind a mechitzah and is not about to start now. And Cousin Serena thinks it's appalling that only men get called to the Torah for aliyos. If they are going to come to your son's bar mitzvah and be miserable or mumble under their breath for two and a half hours, don't feel bad if they decide to show up just to hear your son get his aliyah and then leave, or if they choose to skip the service entirely and join you only for the meal afterward. Make sure to tell them how happy you are that they came, for whatever part they chose to participate in.

ON A PERSONAL NOTE

It was the issue of observant and nonobservant family members attending one another's simchas that originally generated the idea for this book. When I was on the lecture circuit for my book *Two Jews Can Still Be a Mixed Marriage,* I would speak to congregations, sisterhoods, and men's clubs about the challenges in a marriage when one spouse wishes to be more observant than the other. I would typically give a forty-five-minute presentation and then take questions. During the presentation my focus was on the marriage and how to work out issues of kashrus, mikvah, Shabbos, and holidays. But when it came time for questions, several audience members would inevitably raise their hands and (more often than not with some hostility) ask me what I'd recommend in a situation when observant family members won't attend, for example, a wedding or bar or bat mitzvah of a nonobservant family member—or, if they would show up, would not participate in most of the ceremony or the reception afterward.

It was pretty clear to me that the questioners, none of whom was observant, expected me to sympathize with them and assure them that I thought it was terrible of their observant relatives to behave this way. Or they wanted me to give them suggestions for how to convince their observant relatives not to be so stubborn.

I knew from the frequency with which I was being asked this question, and from the hurt and anger so often expressed with it, that a book like this one needed to be written. So I set out to learn more helpful answers than the ones I was extemporaneously offering from the podium. As with all of my books, I had also had a personal, vested interest in this subject, because just as I was getting these questions from others, I was dealing with them myself, in my quandary over how to resolve these conflicts within my own family. These questions are difficult and, quite frankly, they often cannot be resolved to everyone's complete satisfaction. To be honest with you (as I've been throughout this book), this was the chapter I most dreaded writing. But it was also the chapter I was most eager to research in the course of writing this book, because I knew I would learn a few things myself. I knew that this topic would be painful to address, but that it was absolutely essential for me and for many others like me to confront head-on.

TO SUM IT UP

A simchah is a joyous occasion in the life of a family; it's a time to celebrate and not to argue about religious differences. As you've seen, almost all of these differences can be resolved amicably, and you and your family can enjoy spending this time together. There are tensions that inevitably arise during the planning of any simchah, for all sorts of reasons. Jews believe that times of greatest opportunity come with the greatest amount of obstacles!

Six

WHAT DO YOU MEAN, YOU'RE TAKING A BREAK FROM COLLEGE AND GOING TO YESHIVAH?

How to Explain Education Issues

Beginning with the giving of the Torah on Mount Sinai, Jews have been known as the people of the book. Jewish scholarship in the Diaspora continued to flourish during the Early Middle Ages, when much of Europe was plunged into intellectual and artistic decline, and it has continued over the centuries ever since. We are a people known for our interest in both secular and religious knowledge, and for our accomplishments in many fields of professional endeavor. Jews are represented in areas such as medicine, law, and finance at a much higher percentage than they are represented in the population as a whole. This has been a source of great ethnic pride, not to mention material for generations of stand-up comedians.

So when a newly observant young woman tells her parents that she is taking a leave of absence from Harvard Law School and enrolling in a seminary, or a newly observant young man tells his parents that he wants to study in a yeshivah in Israel for a year before starting his studies at Columbia, they should not be surprised when their news is greeted with a considerable lack of enthusiasm—and sometimes outright horror. And, similarly, when a newly observant son tells his parents that he will be sending their grandchildren not to the elite private school that generations of family members have attended but, rather, to a Jewish day school, he should not be surprised when Grandma and Grandpa tell him that he has just destroyed any possibility that his children will be successful in life.

In some ways, the issue of religious education might be even harder to discuss with your family than keeping kosher or observing Shabbos or dressing differently. Those issues can be occasional irritants to your family, but they are not things your parents or grandparents will be perpetually agonizing over. However, the education of children and grandchildren is frequently a family's central concern. Parents who have problems with a newly observant son who eats only kosher and meticulously observes Shabbos and Jewish holidays, or a newly observant daughter who happily covers her hair and sits behind a mechitzah in shul, are somewhat mollified when their child is named director of neurosurgery at a highly respected hospital. But they will be very upset at what they think will be the likely outcome of a young adult spending years of either part- or full-time study in a yeshivah: an adult child who is perpetually dependent on his parents for financial support and who will not be giving his own children the educational advantages and material support that he himself received as a child.

Whether you are a single, newly observant young adult or you are married, newly observant, and with children of your own, education issues may become a serious source of tension between you and your parents. Your siblings and other relatives may also have strong feelings on this subject, but most of your discussions will be with your parents, and it is their disapproval that will affect you the most, so we'll focus on suggestions for how you can talk about this with them. It's not all that different from how you would talk to anyone else about it. Your parents' worries about your education choices will generally fall into three categories: prosperity, prestige, and parochialism.

PROSPERITY CONCERNS

Whether you have decided to postpone the completion of your undergraduate or graduate studies in order to attend a yeshivah, or you plan to spend some time studying in a yeshivah after you have completed your secular education, or you've dropped out of college or graduate school to study in a yeshivah with no intention of resuming your secular studies in the near future, the first thing your parents are going to ask you is, "And exactly how do you expect to make a living?" It's a valid question.

When you tell your parents that you've decided to take your children out of the public or private school they are currently attending and enroll them in a yeshivah or Jewish day school, they will probably say something like, "Your kids will not know how to get along in the real world. They are missing out on a well-rounded education. They won't be able to find a good job." If your children had been attending a public school, your parents might also be concerned about the sizable tuition burden that you will now have to bear—money, they may feel, that should be put away for college and graduate school or that could be spent on vacations or home improvements. In either case, it comes down to two worries rooted in prosperity concerns: (1) they're unaware of the high caliber of both religious and secular instruction in many yeshivas today, and (2) they are concerned that you will expect them to help support you forever, and they may not be completely confident that they will be able to manage their retirement years even without the additional expense of an adult child.

A PREFATORY NOTE

While there are many yeshivas that pride themselves on the percentage of their graduates who wind up in Ivy League schools, there are also yeshivas that, because of their religious philosophy and worldview, provide their students with a superb religious education but with only the most rudimentary secular education, so as to comply with local board of education requirements. They actively discourage their students from pursuing post–high school secular education that is not strictly career-related. If you send your child to this kind of yeshivah, or if you choose to attend this kind of yeshivah instead of the premed program your parents had dreamed about for you, can you blame them for being upset? This reinforces their worst nightmares: that you and/or their grandchildren are being so completely removed from the secular world that any hopes they may have had of your maintaining a connection with your extended family are unrealistic, and any ideas you have about how you will make a living are a fantasy that the rabbi who brainwashed you in the first place has put into your head. If you look at this through their eyes, their anxiety is totally understandable. As we've discussed elsewhere in this book, whether you are explaining to your parents about kashrus, Shabbos, modesty, dating, family simchas, or education, you will need to keep reassuring them that you still love and respect them, that you still very much want to be a part of their lives, and that you are fully aware of the necessity to make a living.

THE ORTHODOX JEWISH DAY SCHOOL AND HIGH SCHOOL SYSTEMS

Because much of your parents' concern comes from not really knowing how Orthodox Jewish day schools, yeshivah high schools, and more advanced yeshivas function, let's start by helping you describe this educational system to them in a more comprehensive way. We'll focus for now on the Orthodox Jewish day schools and high schools that go so far as to take out ads in local Jewish newspapers proudly listing all the prestigious universities that have accepted their graduates. Your parents may not be aware that these schools not only allow but even encourage their students to follow their Jewish day school education with both undergraduate and graduate studies. They probably assume that, because of the emphasis placed on religious studies in yeshivas, students graduating from these schools will have lesser abilities and skills in secular subjects than students who attend public or secular private schools. This is simply not the case, based on years of evidence and thousands of graduating students.

The dual curriculum of religious and secular studies is a rigorous one, but most students not only handle it well, they thrive on it. Half the day is devoted to religious subjects—Bible, Talmud, Jewish law, Jewish history, ethics, etc.—and the other half is devoted to the same secular subjects that are taught in public and private schools. And, yes, there are extracurricular activities, too. Many yeshivah high schools also offer college-level electives.

How do they fit it all in? They start earlier and end later. Most yeshivas start the day at eight-thirty in the morning and end it between an hour and a half and two and a half hours later than public schools. With it all, many yeshivah kids take after-school music and/or art classes and participate in sports programs. How do they do it? You'd be amazed at how much time you have when you cut out a significant amount of television watching and you aren't dating as a teenager! (In fact, keeping teenagers extremely busy with their studies and with extracurricular programs is a well-known strategy to help ensure that they have less of an opportunity to engage in undesirable activities.)

As to the worries that a religious school education is lower in quality than a secular education, standardized tests disprove that theory completely. Yeshivah students score as well as, or even higher than, their secular peers. Small class sizes, committed and caring teachers, separation of boys and girls in the classroom, and strict requirements in the areas of character, ethical behavior, and respect for teachers all contribute to a learning environment that fully leverages the time children spend in the school.

POST–HIGH SCHOOL YESHIVAH EDUCATION

If your parents are accustomed to religious education essentially ending at bar mitzvah, it's hard for them to understand that for the observant Jew, religious education continues through adulthood. To your parents, post–high school yeshivah education is a completely unknown realm. Here's a brief summary of the options available to both men and women, to help you explain to your parents what you are selecting for yourself or for your young adult children.

There are fully accredited yeshivah colleges that offer a dual curriculum in religious and secular studies, and that even have affiliated graduate schools. There are post–high school yeshivas for men and for women (women's yeshivas are commonly referred to as "seminaries") that offer both full-time and part-time programs of religious study and that can accommodate people who want to attend college at the same time. Many colleges will give students elective course credit for classes taken in these yeshivas. There are women's seminaries that offer fully accredited graduate-level degrees in education and related fields, and there are men's yeshivas that maintain educational partnerships with local colleges so that their students can enroll in both undergraduate and graduate programs. Your parents may be surprised to learn that there are more than a few law schools and MBA programs in the United States that will accept students who have spent years studying in a yeshivah and have not attended college at all. These students often score significantly higher than college graduates on GREs, GMATs, and LSATs.

There are also post–high school yeshivas for men that are solely for intensive, full-time religious study and that will not permit their students to attend college at the same time. Their day begins early in the morning with prayer services and can end, with breaks included for breakfast, lunch, and dinner, sometime between 9 and 10 p.m. These yeshivas offer a rigorous program of study that is both intellectually and physically demanding. They are the heirs to the great European yeshivas that were destroyed during the Holocaust, and many bear the names of those vanished institutions, where generations of rabbis—legendary Talmudic scholars and halachic experts—were educated. Some of these yeshivas are located in the United States but even more can be found in Israel. Thousands of young men study in them, some for a few years after high school and before they are ready to enter the business world or resume their secular education; some in preparation for lives devoted to teaching, writing, or serving as pulpit rabbis; and others who have simply decided to devote their lives to Torah study and who have sponsors or family members who are willing to support them and their families.

If you are interested in this type of study program you will need either parents who have the means and desire to support you, or you will need to work out other financial sponsorship arrangements. Many parents of newly observant Jews would probably not be enthusiastic about this option; in fact, it might be just what they are afraid of.

You would know better than I how amenable your parents would be to helping support you, even if you can assure them that you intend to spend only a few years in this type of study and that you will eventually be able to support yourself in some sort of career. There are some parents who would enthusiastically support a child or grandchild's decision to attend this type of yeshivah; there are others who would want no part of it. It's their decision.

YESHIVAS FOR THE NEWLY OBSERVANT

It might be reassuring to your parents to know that there are so many newly observant young adults in situations similar to yours, that special yeshivas have been established for young men and women who did not have an elementary school or high school yeshivah education. You're not the only one who's come up with this strange idea of taking time off from secular studies to attend yeshivah. You've taken a leave from either college or graduate school, or you've finished your secular education and are deferring your entry into the business world so that you can catch up on the years of religious learning—studying the Torah, the Talmud, contemporary Jewish law, the practical aspects of living an observant life—that you did not have when you were younger. How long does it take to get up to observant speed? Religious learning is a lifelong process for anyone, regardless of his or her background. But in practical terms, so that you can give your parents an answer when they want to know how long you will be involved with this, most people spend a year or two of intensive study in these yeshivas before they feel comfortable enough in their knowledge level to either resume their secular studies or their careers, while perhaps continuing with their learning on a part-time basis. Part-time study options are available at these yeshivas, too, as are scholarships for those who need them. Typically, no one is ever turned away for financial reasons.

If your parents are worried that you are entering a yeshivah that turns out cookie-cutter products, an assembly line of strangely garbed people and unified thinking, they'd be surprised to see the interesting mix of men and women who attend these yeshivas. Newly observant Jews can range in age from their early twenties to their sixties, and students have been known to include noted personalities from the business, entertainment, and political worlds. Their levels of religious knowledge vary widely, as do their degrees of religious commitment. It makes for lively encounters and interesting learning sessions.

Even if you are able to reassure your parents that you and your children can be observant and at the same time get a quality education, land a good job, and support a family, they might well have other concerns. What happens when you tell them that what you really want to be is a rabbi of a shul or a yeshivah teacher, or that you want to do part-time consulting work so that you can spend part of your day learning in a yeshivah? What happens when you tell them that you just don't want to reduce the time spent in your Torah studies for the years of intensive study it will take for you to become a doctor, and that you want to become an occupational therapist instead? Maybe your parents dreamed of the party they would throw for you when you got your Columbia MBA and landed that job with a Wall Street firm; instead, they don't know how to explain to their friends what you'll be doing as the sixth-grade rebbe at an all-boys yeshivah. These are not trivial feelings we're dealing with; they are very real, and they must be addressed with respect.

PRESTIGE CONCERNS

Imagine a scenario like this, or substitute a similar one of your own. Your great-grandparents came to the United States at the turn of the last century and perhaps made it through high school. Your grandparents worked during the day and went to college at night during the Depression, or perhaps got their degrees via the GI Bill after World War II. Your parents were the first in the family to have graduate degrees. You've got a brother at Columbia University Law School and a sister at Wharton. And you've just told your parents that you're going to be a Hebrew teacher in a yeshivah. As far as they are concerned, you've just set the family back at least one hundred years.

The problem is, of course, that your parents' definition of having "made it" in America is very different from yours. A great deal of what they define as making it is assimilating and acculturating into mainstream American society and adopting its values. This has been the goal of the vast majority of immigrant Jews and their descendants for the last 350 years, and, frankly, when you were a child you probably reaped the material rewards of their backbreaking commitment to success.

When you are newly observant, you may choose to immerse yourself in your observant life to the point where it even defines what you do for a living. Or, you might very well choose a line of work specifically because it does not interfere with your commitments to Shabbos and holiday observance. If it's hard for your parents to understand why you are observant in the first place, it will be even harder for them to understand why your religious practices also have to determine what you do for a living. If your Jewishness seems to them to stand in the way of your achieving the "American dream" that they have struggled to achieve, you are rejecting something that is very precious to them. Eventually, when they see how happy and fulfilled you are in what you are doing and in the way you are living your life, and when they see how beautifully your children have turned out and how much nachas they give their grandparents, they may well become as proud of you as they are of your siblings. It's not fair, though, to expect this of them right away. If you look at this through their eyes, the choices you are making in life look problematic to them; only time may show them otherwise.

To better understand how your family may be feeling about your choosing a profession that is defined by your Jewish observance, we enter into the realm of what some might call becoming "too Jewish." To some more assimilated or acculturated Jews, Judaism is something to celebrate privately, or with other Jewish friends in your home or synagogue. But does the rest of the world have to define you by the fact that you are Jewish? Is there perhaps a feeling among some of your relatives that you've become "too Jewish?"

To get a handle on this concept of "too Jewish," let's see if we can understand what might be at the root of your parents' concerns. Are they concerned about your religious beliefs? Probably not, if you don't impose these beliefs on them. But Judaism is more than a religious belief. We're also a nation, a people joined together by a common history, culture, language, and land. Jews live all over the world now, but your parents may be worried that if you become "too Jewish," you might, for example, move to Israel, and then they'll hardly ever see you or their grandchildren. That's an understandable concern. Are they put off by the way you and your family look? The yarmulke, the tzitzis, the beard, the conservative dress, the outward appearance of an Orthodox Jew. Is all this "too Jewish" for them?

For two thousand years, Jews have been living their lives in reaction to the non-Jewish societies in which they have found themselves, and they have been redefining what it means to be Jewish within those societies. To be fair to your family, the well-grounded fear of anti-Semitism and the desire to live peacefully within the non-Jewish world explain why many Jews throughout history have chosen to deemphasize public displays of their Jewishness. What is meant by "too Jewish"? It is an expression that articulates the age-old Jewish fear of anti-Semitism, the belief that assimilation is a form of protection that must not be stripped away. If we intentionally stick out too much, we are being ungrateful to our "host country" and something bad will happen to us. Lurking behind your parents' alarm over the lack of prestige of your chosen profession is something else. They are worried about you and your family. If you are a law professor, you show that you are willing to blend into the professional world around you. If you are a yeshivah rebbe, with a beard and peyos and tzitzis, you are declaring to the world around you that you are Jewish—perhaps "too Jewish" to the people who want to keep you safe and who worry about anti-Semitism, even here in America.

Even nowadays, some Jews measure their success by how well they fit in within the non-Jewish world around them. The Jew who takes pride in his traditions and feels no need to downplay them to the rest of the world—steadfastly holding on to his beard, his peyos, and his tzitzis—can be a source of embarrassment, and not nachas, to his family. Your parents may consider it a badge of honor if you become a tenured professor of English, French, or German literature. But should you choose to become a Torah scholar, while this will be a source of great pride to your wife and your children, your parents may feel differently. It might take them a while until they get to the point where they are proud of an endeavor they may have thought was either a waste of time or something that they felt uncomfortable proclaiming to the outside world.

Observant Jews are too proud of their eternal heritage to be preoccupied with fitting into a secular world with ever-changing values. But we do live in this secular world, and we must be able to relate to and understand people who live outside of the religious community. This brings us to the third objection your parents may have about a yeshivah education.

PAROCHIALISM CONCERNS

"Your children won't be exposed to the outside world in which they will eventually have to live. They will be unable to understand other cultures, and if they attend an all-boys or all-girls yeshivah they won't have the skills to relate to the opposite sex." These are some of the objections your parents may voice when you tell them that you've decided to send your kids to a Jewish day school or a yeshivah. They will be concerned that your children's education, which is supposed to prepare them for life, will produce sheltered people who will be unable to function in the "real" world as adults. They may also feel that educating them solely among other Jews (or, even worse, among only other observant Jews) will result in their being narrow-minded and unable to see any value in other cultures.

If your parents raise this objection, try explaining to them that observant Jews send their children to Jewish schools so that they can learn about Judaism *in addition* to learning about secular subjects, not instead of it. We live in a society that bombards us with information about the world we live in, whether it's via magazines and newspapers or television and radio or the Internet. As a result of the media attention surrounding Mel Gibson's movie, people have learned more about Christianity than they would otherwise know. As a result of the horrific events that occurred on 9/11, people know more about Islam than they would otherwise know. Jewish parents who want their children to be knowledgeable about their religion—its history, its values, its rituals—have to provide them with a Jewish education in addition to a secular education. How best to do this?

There are those who feel that a few hours of religious instruction on Sundays and one or two days during the week until age thirteen will suffice, but observant Jews don't feel that way. They feel that there are thousands of years of Jewish knowledge that they want to transmit to their children, and that the only way to begin to accomplish this is by sending their children to a Jewish day school and giving them the opportunity to spend half of their school day focused on Judaic learning. Remind your parents that children who attend a synagogue-based Hebrew school for a few hours a week are for the most part preparing for a bar or bat mitzvah and not a life of observance. There simply aren't enough after-school hours to teach observant Jewish children all they need to know to live observant Jewish lives as adults.

Your parents are probably well aware of the many social problems facing American teenagers today, including drug and alcohol abuse, and teenage pregnancy. Being in a yeshivah environment is not, of course, a panacea for every teenage crisis, but a child who attends a yeshivah will be less exposed to the social problems that plague young people. Your parents will probably find it hard to completely disagree with this. As far as the value of interacting with children from other cultures is concerned, this is where you and your parents might simply have to disagree. They may feel that in our multicultural society, it's important to expose young children, in a classroom setting, to children with other belief systems or with no belief system at all. Observant Jews disagree. If your kids are educated with the right set of values in a yeshivah, when they encounter the outside world as young adults they will have no problem interacting with people from different backgrounds. And observing how you—and your parents—interact with people from different cultural and religious backgrounds in the course of daily life will teach them a lot more than they could learn in any public school classroom. Your parents may never completely agree with you about this, but, ultimately, if your kids turn out happy and healthy and successful, they'll relax about it.

It may interest your parents to know that at more than a few large corporations in the Greater New York area, there are enough observant Jews employed so that they can, with the permission of the corporation, hold a daily minyan on the company premises. These yeshivah-educated men don't seem to have had any difficulty adjusting to life in the outside world, and neither will your child. More often than not, an observant Jew is treated with particular respect in the business and professional worlds.

More so than any other issue discussed in this book, your parents' concerns about how you are educating your children will resolve themselves over time, when they see their grandchildren creating their own stable, financially secure, happy Jewish homes. Unlike keeping kosher or observing Shabbos, which your parents may simply not see the need for, their concerns about your children's education relate to their concerns over what sort of kids their grandchildren are going to be. If you succeed in raising respectful, happy, and accomplished children, your parents will see that they have nothing to worry about. Which doesn't necessarily mean that they won't continue to worry, but perhaps not as much.

ON A PERSONAL NOTE

As the parents of young children, Stephen and I have been driven by one primary concern when choosing a place to live: Where do we want to educate our children? Because we know we want yeshivah educations for our children from nursery through high school and beyond, we can't live just anywhere in the United States. Where we live has to be within a reasonable driving distance to yeshivas that we feel comfortable sending our children to and also a reasonable driving distance to an area where Stephen can find employment. (I work from home, so I'm more portable.)

Could we compromise? Which is to say, enroll our kids in a Jewish day school that doesn't reflect our level of observance, or send them to public school and hire after-school tutors in Jewish subjects, or enrich their lives with the best Jewish summer camp we can find? We'd save thousands of dollars a year in tuition. Paying what we do for tuition, which starts in preschool, places a great deal of financial pressure on us. But this is what we want to do. Actually, we feel that this is what we *must* do. It's as important to us as making sure that the children are eating healthy food, kept safe, and receive regular medical check-ups. For us, the question never is, "*Should* we send the kids to a Jewish day school" but, rather, "Which school is best, and how will we pay for it?"

Perhaps this conviction is due in part to the fact that Stephen and I both attended public schools as children and that I didn't receive a Jewish education as a child. Or maybe it's seeing how beautifully our children have turned out with the few years of Jewish education that they already have experienced. They have a love for Torah and a pride in their Judaism that brings tears to my eyes. Actually, it's more than that. It feels like a religious obligation, that this is my responsibility as a Jewish parent. Just as I wouldn't feed them nonkosher food, I wouldn't send my kids to anything but a yeshivah, even if it means forgoing a lot of material comforts that we would otherwise have been able to afford. I am not saying that every Jew should make this decision. What I am saying is this: The priority that Stephen and I place on educating our children in yeshivas is one of the governing values of our lives. It is never an "if" question, only a "how."

The beauty of our current home is not reflected in the yard (which is practically nonexistent), or in the spaciousness of the house (which is definitely not its best feature), or in the congested streets that make bike-riding problematic for the children. The beauty of our home is in what Stephen and I see every day when our kids come home from yeshivah and share with us their love for Torah, their excitement about their studies, and their pride in being observant Jews. It's in the scene on Shabbos, when the streets fill with Jews going to and from synagogue and to one another's homes for Shabbos lunch. It's when we feel such joy and pride in the people our children are becoming that our decision to shape our lives around their yeshivah education makes any sense at all.

AFTERWORD

I have grown tremendously from writing this book, in both knowledge and gratitude, because I see how painful these family disagreements can be and because I have also witnessed the true healing and harmony that can be achieved. I have learned that more can be done than I ever imagined to bridge the gap between observant and less- or nonobservant family members. I have also come to respect the limits of what can be achieved, and to accept that within my family there are limits to what I can share with relatives whose perspectives on religious matters are so different from mine. It's good to hope for better, but it's also realistic to accept what is. I continue to ask God for help, clarity, and healing.

I hold in my heart a prayer that you and your family can find the path of shalom bayis, and that when tensions arise (and they will) you will be able to summon the courage and respect to deal with one another in a way that strengthens your family rather than destroys it. Let the Torah be a guide for how to love one another, and don't let difficult times discourage you. The glue that holds families together is very strong, even when pulled from opposite directions.

Don't stop communicating with your family—it shows that you care. Agreeing to disagree is still better than maintaining a polite distance. Stubbornly hold on to your vision of family harmony, even when it seems to elude you. Never, under any circumstances, say "Never!" We all dream of close-knit, loving, and mutually respectful families. Even if it seems impossible at times, with God's help, amazing things can happen when family members are dedicated to sticking it out through the difficult times and learning from one another. I'd be more than happy to hear from you with your questions, and to hear your personal stories and the successes you have achieved. You can reach me at azjaffe@optonline.net.

May each of you find the patience, insight, and love to transform strife into shalom bayis, and sadness into nachas. And may God bless all of our households with peace. Shalom bayis begins at home. May it reside in yours, and in that of your extended family.

About the Author

Azriela Jaffe is the author of twelve previously published books, including *Two Jews Can Still Be a Mixed Marriage,* which was an alternate selection of the Jewish Book Club. She is also the publisher and author of *After the Diet: Delicious Kosher Recipes with Less Fat, Calories, and Carbs,* and of a forthcoming novel, *A Change of Heart.* She lives in Highland Park, New Jersey, with her husband and three children. She welcomes responses from readers at azjaffe@optonline.net. Visit her on the Web at www.azriela.com.

A Note on the Type

This book was set in Minion, a typeface produced by the Adobe Corporation specifically for the Macintosh personal computer, and released in 1990. Designed by Robert Slimbach, Minion combines the classic characteristics of old style faces with the full compliment of weights required for modern typesetting.

Composed by Creative Graphics,
Allentown, Pennsylvania
Printed and bound by R. R. Donnelley & Sons,
Harrisonburg, Virginia
Designed by M. Kristen Bearse